THE SECOND ARROW

AMITABH RAY

INDIA • SINGAPORE • MALAYSIA

Notion Press

No.8, 3rd Cross Street
CIT Colony, Mylapore
Chennai, Tamil Nadu – 600004

First Published by Notion Press 2020
Copyright © Amitabh Ray 2020
All Rights Reserved.

ISBN 978-1-63606-648-6

This book has been published with all efforts taken to make the material error-free after the consent of the author. However, the author and the publisher do not assume and hereby disclaim any liability to any party for any loss, damage, or disruption caused by errors or omissions, whether such errors or omissions result from negligence, accident, or any other cause.

While every effort has been made to avoid any mistake or omission, this publication is being sold on the condition and understanding that neither the author nor the publishers or printers would be liable in any manner to any person by reason of any mistake or omission in this publication or for any action taken or omitted to be taken or advice rendered or accepted on the basis of this work. For any defect in printing or binding the publishers will be liable only to replace the defective copy by another copy of this work then available.

Contents

Prologue: The Happiness Code	5
1. Embracing Uncertainty – A Survival Kit	7
2. The Age of Chaos and Creativity	19
3. Life Isn't Fair, but You Don't Have to be Unfair	31
4. Walk a Mile in Someone Else's Shoes	43
5. Have Never Arrived: The Zone of Comfortable Discomfort	53
6. Gen Z: Post-COVID Tech Transformation on Steroids	67
7. A COVID-Normal Future – Accept, Adapt and Stay Agile	75
8. The Day of the Authentic Leader	83
9. I Have No Plans and No Plans to Plan	93
10. Theory of Relativity – The Emergency	109
11. Doing the Right Things vs. Doing Things Right	119
12. Being Always Right is Never Right	133
13. Three Transformations, Three Journeys	141
14. Thinking of Possibilities Critically	157

15. The View from a Vantage Point	163
16. A Sudden Chance to Change the Status Quo	169
17. Building India Next	185
18. The Story of the Second Arrow	191
Epilogue: Mississippi Morphs into Ganga	*193*

Prologue: The Happiness Code

My life began by the banks of the river Ganga in a sleepy town on the northern fringes of the city of Kolkata. I loved the river and still fondly remember the joy of splashing around in its lap with youthful abundance. Back then, the world was different.

A lot of water has flown ever since. When I started working on this book, I tried to figure out why I was doing it. I do this every time I begin a piece of work. Once the purpose is clear, the rest falls in place and the big picture emerges. All along, I keep questioning myself with an open mind – trying to figure out how people with better ideas would have done it.

I realized I wanted to look back on the flow of my life – to document it in a way through which a coherent message might emerge. And that could serve as a course-correction guide for my days ahead.

Essentially, three streams of thoughts emerged as I reflected. The first was de-focusing from being conscious of success and winning. If I removed 'winning' from everything we did, then work became enjoyable. Success would be a natural outcome of a job well done – this was my Happiness

Code. Life and work can become enjoyable if we have 'Being Happy' as the objective and not winning or being successful; these are automatic byproducts of being happy.

The second thought was about the burden of expectations on our shoulders. When I started, I was not expected to achieve anything specific, and so there was nothing to weigh me down. That gave me incredible freedom to take the plunge whenever I had to.

And finally, there was the parable of the second arrow. We will talk more about that by the end of this book. But it is all about our responses to misfortune or setback and how we could control that to shape our destiny.

We live in a world buffeted by ceaseless changes and paradoxes. But over time, I realized that the more things changed, the more they remained the same. I looked back at changes that have happened in the past, and how things eventually went back to normal – making change a part of life. We all live by juggling paradoxes, sometimes even without realizing it. Leadership, too, is often faced with the dilemma of whether to take the lead or to recede into the background.

A post-Covid world is certainly going to be different, and yet the principles of honesty, humility, dedication, and being in control of our responses – will always hold true amidst an ocean of transformation. You can never bathe in the same river twice because the flowing waters keep shifting every moment, yet the river stays the same.

Chapter 1

Embracing Uncertainty – A Survival Kit

*I*revisited a few chapters once I was finalizing the book that I had started writing almost a year before COVID-19 hit the world. To my surprise, I found that it needed very few changes. I was writing about uncertainty and how to embrace it. Nothing has changed, except that the velocity of uncertainty has increased exponentially. As you read this chapter, you'll come across this sentence: "In the next five years, by 2025, the rate of automation of jobs will increase dramatically. For every hour of some jobs, 48% of it will be performed by humans while 52% will be done by machines, as per a World Economic Forum study." The only thing I want to change was the timespan. Instead of five years, I would say that automation is going to happen in the next two to three years or even less. The need to maintain physical distancing has created a whole new model, Distance Dynamics of Remote Everything, which has fast-forwarded the digital transformation of every enterprise. This, in turn, will need us to develop a new set of skills to stay relevant. Everything that we said would take a decade or five years to happen will now happen much faster; that's the only change we must factor in.

***

I sat sipping oversweet tea from an earthenware cup on the hand-pumped four-wheeled section car used to inspect railroad tracks at the end of the Berhampur railway station in Odisha. Charminar was the cheapest cigarette I could afford. I went there every evening to watch the Madras Mail on its way to Calcutta, wistfully gazing at the faces of the passengers on their way to my city. *One day, I'll take this train back home*, I told myself. I was a homesick young man trying to get an MBA from a rather average management institute in Berhampur as my passport to a career.

I didn't have what it took, in terms of merit, to seek admission in an IIM. My mentor, teacher and almost elder brother, Dr Samir Sadhukhan, a brilliant doctor of engineering and a faculty at IIM-Calcutta, was a well-meaning and candid person. He had my best interests in his heart when he told me not to waste time trying to get into an IIM and instead explore a tier two or three institute to add an MBA to my curriculum vitae. For an arts graduate with a diploma in computers, an MBA was my only realistic shot at making a career. So here I was in Berhampur, longing every moment to get back home to my friends, football and acting in local plays.

My coach who taught me compassion

Dr Sadhukhan was my coach and taught me computer programming at his home. Like any other young graduate in the early eighties, we all tried to learn some amount of programming – an emerging career option. It was the good professor who instilled in me a passion for computers. A diploma in computers and an MBA would be my survival weapon in the coming era, which will witness unprecedented changes, he advised me.

I had no option but to make myself ready for a digital future that was already unfolding; otherwise, it was the gloom of uncertainty that faced me. He gave me my first lesson of life – acquiring new skills was the only mantra for survival in an uncertain world. Sometimes, we are lucky to be in the right place at the right time, although that happens very rarely. Most of the time, we must create the right place and take up a position, like an intelligent footballer who knows exactly where the pass will come.

On my way back from the station to the hostel, I saw a cloth banner outside a rundown shop. It had a rather overambitious signage that bragged – 'National Computer Center'. Curiosity gripped me as I pushed open the rickety doors to find a man lying on a wobbly cot in an empty room. It was obviously a shop that had run out of business. Ranjit Pattanaik, the man on the cot, lazily got up and introduced himself as the owner of the National Computer Center and asked me what I wanted. I offered him my services as a programming trainer for his center and told him that I could help him set it up. For a paltry sum of Rs 200 a month, I took up the evening job, teaching computer skills to students after my college hours. My aim was to keep my skills polished as the money didn't even cover my rickshaw fare to the center from my institute.

My first IT job

Business soon became brisk, and Pattanaik was happy. We even started taking on some development work from nearby factories that used to give 'Data Processing' work to information technology (IT) companies in big cities like Bhubaneshwar and Calcutta. Thus began my humble experience in IT outsourcing and development work.

My lesson learned was, opportunity happened to those who went looking for it and worked hard toward it. I had created the right place for myself and the time became right through hard work. Pushing open the doors of the National Computer Center was lucky for me, but luck, I learned that day, was self-made. I could easily have turned away from a ramshackle shop with no customers. What made me walk in was perhaps my feeling that nothing was too small for me to work on. In later years, nothing was too big for me to attempt.

The center gave me hands-on experience in running projects. I earned and learned at the same time. I told my batchmates, who kidded me on the meager money Pattanaik paid me, that one day I would turn this Rs 200 into a Rs 2000-a-month job. Back in those days, Rs 2000 was a princely sum, especially for someone with my qualifications. In fact, my first job paid me Rs 2500. It was a small company called ACE that later changed its name to SQL Star.

Hands-on project experience will be the differentiator today as organizations will no longer look for certificates of academic qualifications only. They will prefer talent with the right skills to do the job. Some of the Big Four consulting firms have announced that a college degree is no longer an essential criterion for a job in their organizations – skills mattered more than degrees. Apple, Google and Netflix do not require employees to have four-year degrees, and this could soon become an industry norm. LinkedIn found that many of today's hottest US companies do not require a college degree but the ability to quickly learn and use new skills. We have entered the Age of Lifelong Learning and we are going to have a great time continuously learning in the classroom of life and work. This is Liquid Learning. This is the art of staying relevant, which will need us to be adaptive, agile and analytical.

Whenever I got stuck with a difficult bit of programming while delivering projects for the National Computer Center, I rushed to Dr Sadhukhan for help, which he delightedly offered. From him, I learned that helping others selflessly created an enormous bank of goodwill. It mattered then, and it made a huge difference today, in a networked society, where collaboration and teamwork were key to survival and success in an increasingly connected world.

Learn, unlearn, relearn

The kind professor didn't have to help me, but he did it because he possessed – like all good individuals – a precious quality called compassion. It means walking a mile in another person's shoes. He went out of his way to help his students. For him, solving any intellectual challenge was an opportunity to keep himself at the edge of knowledge. He was a lifelong learner as he strongly believed that it was the only way to stay relevant in a turbulent world. This was a huge lesson for me from my teacher and mentor.

If what you learn today is redundant in a couple of years, then the only way to survive is to learn, unlearn what you've learned and relearn new skills. According to the World Economic Forum, 75 million current job roles may be displaced by the shift in the division of labor between humans, machines and algorithms, while 133 million new job roles may emerge at the same time. This will happen as companies adopt new technologies like high-speed mobile internet, artificial intelligence, big data analytics, edge computing, cloud technology and robotics, among several others. This has already started, hastened by the once-in-a-century event of a pandemic.

Empathy at the center of design thinking

Jobs like a cab driver, a drone pilot, an artificial intelligence engineer, a technology ethicist, a YouTuber, a driverless car engineer, a social media consultant or a user experience engineer didn't exist a couple of years ago. Each of these requires a different set of skills from what we're being trained for today. Empathy is the very basis of a user experience designer that will require a high level of design thinking. It will essentially mean putting the customer and the user at the center of every product or service and imagining how they will use and interact with those. As the internet of things becomes mission-critical and everything becomes connected, building interactivity into a design will be central. Skills required will be different in a zero contact, remote everything world.

Critical thinking will be one of the most sought-after skills as we will be required to cope with solving not just problems but paradoxes. A problem can be clearly defined and there exists a solution. But a paradox is often couched in ambiguity and a solution to it will give rise to another bigger problem. Most of the time, it has multiple solutions to the same problem and there are no right answers. For instance, the more the world develops, the more natural resources we consume and contribute to global warming. So which option do you choose? Stop development to halt global warming or look for sustainable solutions?

The next level of HR challenge will be figuring out systems and processes to evaluate human-robot collaborative work. I can foresee a supervisor for robots as an emerging job. HR data detectives will soon be a much sought-after job as well, which will require people to connect dots and find correlations. According to a recent study by Harvard Business Review, "for HR professionals, the future of work will include developing a stronger focus and a more holistic view of employee wellbeing, one that encompasses the emotional, mental and spiritual health of workers along with the physical". It even mentions the role of a Director of Wellbeing, who could provide strategic management over wellness and design services and practices to nurture the emotional, physical, mental and spiritual health of all employees.

Some years ago, while speaking to a group of students at an IIM event, I saw the shock and disbelief writ large on their faces when I told them that a substantial part of what they learned in the first year would become redundant by the time they left the institute some four years down the line. Over the next 20 years, or maybe even earlier, we will be seeing more changes than what we had witnessed in the last 200 years. Several jobs that we will do in 2030 haven't been invented yet.

The lifecycle of technologies is rapidly collapsing, and new technologies are being introduced even before the existing ones had run their full course.

The world continues to change fast, and one won't be able to catch up if one does not stay updated. Companies like Samsung are disrupting their own products. Even Moore's Law is being disrupted. More than 50 years after Intel founder, Gordon Moore, said that the number of transistors that could fit on a silicon chip would double every two years, physical constraints are preventing the cramming of more transistors on smaller pieces of silicon.

Intel cautioned some time ago that its transistors would stop shrinking by 2021. It has meanwhile found a new way of 3D chip stacking on top of each other to keep increasing computing power, while Nvidia is producing a GPU (Graphic Processing Unit) to enhance processing speed. Even before you pause to take a breath, Quantum Computing is promising to incredibly transform computing.

Taiwan Semiconductor Manufacturing Company (TSMC) has already launched 5 nanometer (nm) semiconductors and is currently working on 3nm. Compared to 7nm (N7) technology, N5 technology offers about 15% speed improvement or about 30% reduction in power consumption. N3 will be another full node stride over N5 with a density improvement of 1.7x. Initial estimates for the N3 predict that it will offer a cell-level density of just under 300 million transistors per millimeter square. A nanometer is one-billionth of a meter, 0.000000001 or 10-9 meters. To put things into perspective, a human hair is about 60,000 – 100,000 nm wide. It is obvious that transformations are now happening at a level that no average human mind could even conceive, going by everyday logic!

Industrial revolutions are happening faster than ever

5G is already ushering in incredible possibilities that will transform our lives and businesses. Everything from driverless cars to remote surgery will be possible through millimeter waves. Founded only six years ago, Carbon3D, a 3D printer-making company, is now a $1-billion startup working with automobile companies, like Ford, and healthcare giants, such as Johnson & Johnson, literally reshaping manufacturing, healthcare, automotive, retail and so on.

If you look at the time gap between the first and second industrial revolutions, it was approximately 100 years – the same as it was between the second and third revolutions. It took just half the time for the fourth revolution to start after the third. Five companies – Microsoft, Facebook, Amazon, Disney and Apple – dominate the Standard & Poor index, accounting for 30% of its gain in the first half of 2019.

If you notice the composition of the list, four are technology companies and the oldest among them is Microsoft, which is only 44 years old, Apple is just a year younger, and Amazon is 25 years old, while Facebook is still a teenager at 15, and YouTube is only 14 years old. The first-ever picture uploaded on Instagram was of a dog by the co-founder of this app, Kevin Systrom. He shared the photo on July 16, 2010; three months later, in October, it was launched to the public. Gone are the dominant oil and gas companies and great industrial behemoths from the top ten. For the first time in 100 years, ExxonMobil was no longer in the top-ten list of the S&P Index.

In the next five years or so, the rate of automation of jobs will increase dramatically. For every hour of a job, 48% of it will be performed by humans while 52% will be done by machines, as per a World Economic Forum study. This will mean a shift in skills. Humans will be required to perform tasks that need more critical thinking, creativity, originality, collaboration and a high level of innovation. Complex problem solving skills, emotional intelligence and empathy will be the key requirements from our future workforce.

Rather disappointingly, these skills are still not a part of the curriculum in our schools and colleges. Our teachers, sincere as they are, use the outdated syllabus. As a result, students are not being trained on the skills they will need to navigate the future of work. I delved into my own experience with what I needed to survive in the workplace after completing my academics.

Our education didn't teach the skills we needed

Oh, how I wished I was trained in soft skills, like communication, making a presentation, conducting a negotiation, functioning in a collaborative environment or being taught that innovation, too, is process-driven. These practical workplace skills require a high level of emotional quotient (EQ) as opposed to IQ, which is essential in doing well in schools and colleges. In my view, skills driven by EQ will be in greater demand in the future of work, regardless of the level of the corporate hierarchy one functions in. No one taught us how to handle failure and yet most of the time, we faced disappointments and rejections. Our wins were few and far between.

In the years when we were growing up, the term 'Emotional Intelligence' didn't exist. A 'good' leader was someone who had high IQ, knowledge, communication and decision-making skills. The term Emotional Intelligence was coined by behavioral researchers, Peter Salovey and John D. Mayer, only in 1990.

These are different times. Success definitions now highlight a new need for understanding, interpreting and managing and using emotions, both our own and those of others. This is the domain of Emotional Intelligence or Emotional Quotient. People always respond to emotional cues. It's as simple as that which makes emotional intelligence such a highly valued leadership attribute. A genuine smile, a frown, a shrug, eyes that speak, are all non-verbal communication that triggers an emotional reaction in others. Likewise, verbal signals like authentic appreciation, compassionate understanding or a social connection do the same. All this whittles down to a simple five-letter word: Trust!

Why is EQ important? It's because emotions bond people. Because human nature hasn't really changed. Because the arrival of Artificial Intelligence has paradoxically made Emotional Intelligence very important.

In fact, the traditional boxes and arrows hierarchy will cease to exist and be replaced by flexible models. This will require people to team up to pool their skills required to deliver a piece of work and then dismantle and re-group with other members for another assignment. A leader in one project could be a team member in another assignment and vice-versa; all determined by the skill levels. This will make our current corporate titles somewhat useless.

Technology will transform how we work. The future of work will be more collaborative as platforms will allow us to create virtual and real teams across vast geographic boundaries seamlessly. This will mean that skills like cultural sensitivity, communication and collaborative ways of working and clear articulation of business value propositions are going to be essential and even spell the difference between success and failure.

As I see these changes in the horizon, some of which are already happening in the workplace, I rummaged through my experience of over three decades and figured out that we have always lived and survived in a chaotic world. From the early days of outsourcing to the Y2K boom, through to the dotcom bust and the great financial meltdown, I have battled, struggled, survived and reinvented myself, though a bit bruised in the journey.

Skills that mattered – embracing uncertainty

I worked through the ranks in my first major professional job at PricewaterhouseCoopers (PwC), one of the Big Four consulting firms, holding all job titles, starting from the bottom of the pyramid as an associate consultant and rising to become a partner and a board member. I continued as a board member in my subsequent roles at IBM and Ericsson, the last of which I currently hold today. In each organization, I was part of teams, led teams and decided on strategies that would eventually transform these companies, all of them over a century old.

In every organization, I discovered that the most powerful tools to survive and succeed, in every situation, regardless of whether one was a junior employee or a board member, were collaboration, teamwork, empathy, creativity, innovation, a problem solving attitude, conflict resolution, critical thinking and an innovative spirit. Technologies were different in each organization. From consulting to IT outsourcing and telecom, the technology landscape changed but what remained constant were these skills. These became my life's lessons.

In the following pages, I'll hold your hand and walk you through my experiences to let you feel what will help you get through some of the most challenging yet exhilarating times we're passing through. I took up writing this book as I felt that I could, in my humble way, tell stories about how these skills that I spoke about mattered more than academic success.

I am not belittling the scorecards that have helped you secure prized jobs in this industry. What I want my readers to understand is that the world is changing, yet certain old-fashioned values are staging a comeback as we grapple with unprecedented challenges. These values were somehow deep-rooted in the way we lived our lives from childhood.

Living with uncertainty has become even more relevant today in a COVID-normal world. We do not know how long this pandemic will disrupt our lives. We have no option but to make disruption, ambiguity, extreme volatility and ever-increasing complexities a part of our lives. My purpose in writing this book will be fulfilled if it helps you figure out how to ride and enjoy these massive waves of transformation coming at us instead of being engulfed by those. This, you can say, is a survival kit to embracing uncertainty!

Chapter 2

The Age of Chaos and Creativity

Years ago, around the late nineties, when I was well-settled in a great job in the US, I decided to take a U-turn and come back home to India. I had gone through a lot of challenges to reach where I had, and exactly at that point in time, when things look settled, I was thinking of giving it up and going back home. Naturally, it didn't make sense to many.

It surprised quite a few of my friends and left some in my family, whose lives I was disrupting, rather bewildered. If they were upset, they certainly didn't show it. But I could make out the lurking unease, tinged perhaps with a degree of frustration at my decision. Once again, I was perhaps unsettling their comfortable lives. But I must confess that they put up a brave face.

Let's admit it, life in the United States of America, especially for qualified Indians in the technology sector with a good job, is almost as perfect as it can get, except, of course, you missed your parents and the friends you grew up with, which I did a lot. Especially for me, because I was attached to my childhood friends, which I still am.

Life was orderly. The weather in the Bay Area, where I was living, suited us fine. We didn't have to face the sweat and grime of back home. We didn't face the challenges of getting our children admitted to good schools. We had good homes and our savings looked handsome when multiplied by the exchange rate. The six-lane highways were an absolute delight to drive in the latest automobiles, and I loved driving and still do.

Our weekend get-togethers with friends were spent discussing our next holidays and the future of our work. It was in one of those evenings when the conversation veered around to going back to India to work in the technology sector, which was, in my opinion, showing promising signs of emerging as a major economic force.

Inviting chaos into my life

It was at that point in time I spoke aloud about my eventual plans to return to India and build and run an SAP practice, as was offered by the organization. A friend of mine, certainly a well-wisher, was dumbstruck at my decision to pack up and leave for India. Once he failed to talk me out of my decision, he quipped in his usual humorous way, "Well, you will run a practice, and we will run our BMWs here."

He didn't expect my response when I said, "Well, what if I also drive one back home?"

He must have felt that I was an extremely cocky fella and perhaps a wee bit overconfident of my capabilities. He certainly had the right to, after all my college education was in history from Rastraguru Surendranath College, a rather humble institution in Barrackpore, in the northern suburbs of Kolkata, and my MBA was from a non-elite university. What must have played in his mind is that without an engineering or an Ivy League management degree, how could I think of making it in India where the competition was tough and merit was measured in terms of academic qualifications alone, despite it being an utterly unprofessional thing to do.

What spurred my decision was my firm conviction that India was the place where frugal innovation was changing things. It was the testbed of innovative home-grown solutions to our local problems that had the potential to become global winners. India was talking about affordable solutions to our problems. Our talent was in finding unique workarounds to challenges. We had learned to focus on the core of the issue, just like the Maruti ad some years back, when even the well-heeled buyer asked: "*Kitna deti hai?*" (How much does it run per liter?). In one of the ad films, travelers were shown entering a state-of-the-art sci-fi aircraft. It was the aircraft's first maiden voyage from London to New York to be covered in three hours, as announced by the attendant. An Indian was shown to be visibly impressed with the aircraft. Air hostesses explained the different features of the aircraft, including virtual reality windows, and said that the crew could speak in 12 different languages. At this point, the Indian calls out in Hindi, leaving the hostesses flabbergasted: "*Kitna deti hai?*"

Maruti Suzuki India Limited (MSIL) had hit the nail on the head with its '*Kitna deti hai*' advertising campaigns. No one knew the Indians' obsession with cost and mileage better than the country's top passenger car manufacturer. It was all about creating our competitive advantage with home-grown solutions. Maruti was iconic of India's transformation. It was a disruptor that everyone was waiting for.

In the early nineties, India's cryogenic engine development program for space research encountered a huge roadblock when international sanctions stalled technology transfer after India tested its nuclear capabilities in Rajasthan's Pokhran. This stumbling block was turned into a stepping-stone by our talented scientists at the Indian Space Research Organization (ISRO), who developed indigenous technology that now powers our rockets and has propelled the country to be a major player in the commercial launch of satellites.

Turning obstacles into opportunities

I remember a report in a financial daily about how a small engineering firm in the outskirts of my hometown, Calcutta, was selected by the ISRO to supply a key technology component. This was trickle-down technology having a cascading effect on the country's progress. India turned a geopolitical disruption into an advantage. The world's business and economic history are replete with such fine examples and even as we face global trade conflicts today, we must figure out how to use these situations to our advantage and create new value propositions.

The MNCs had also noticed the possibilities of leveraging Indian talent and their native skills in frugal innovation. It was in 1985 that Texas Instruments had opened its R&D center in Wind Tunnel Road in Bangalore. Some say that this was the genesis of the Indian IT revolution that swept the world. Others were working on reverse innovation. Global companies were using India as the place to customize and develop products for the local market, blending affordability with international quality. This innovation was then taken to other parts of the world. India and China had the world's largest markets and it made sense to create products for these markets.

It was about my firm conviction that India was changing and was the place to be in. Being in the right place at the right time was not an accident but a deliberate choice of the informed and uncluttered mind, which has a panoramic view of things. I think I have been fortunate in the sense that the right opportunities came to me, which others read as challenges. But I plunged into them, spurred on by my desire to explore, experiment and figure out how to solve problems that others gave up on. You can also influence being in the right place at the right time. All you need is the courage to experiment and have self-belief; it happened to me several times. It is just like how a footballer knows where the ball will go and then positions himself accordingly to kick it into the net. I will talk about this in the following chapters.

You can win the world from India, that's what I felt. The apparent chaos of India was but an outward expression of a surge of creativity trying to break free and change the way things are. A change that was years in the making was now about to unleash itself. Actually, it was more than a change; it was a transformation! The status quo was being challenged.

Bits and Atoms

The first hint of this change came to me when I had the good fortune of listening to Dr Nicholas Negroponte, the founder of MIT Labs. He spoke about bits and atoms. Atoms, he said, were physical things while bits were digitally made up of zeros and ones. The world, he said, knew how to value atoms but would soon unlock the value of bits. Companies declared their atoms on a balance sheet and depreciated them as per rigorous schedules. But isn't it strange that their bits weren't recorded anywhere even though they were mostly far more valuable? It might sound even stranger today that there was a time when music and movies were shipped only as physical objects – atoms!

The MIT professor narrated an anecdote way back in 1995 in a speech titled *The $400-Limit, Applies to Atoms Only*. He said that a US national, when returning from abroad, must complete a customs declaration form in which one must declare the value of physical objects but never the intellectual content in objects, such as a laptop or a diskette. Prof. Negroponte said, "Have customs officers inquired whether you have a diskette worth hundreds of thousands of dollars? No. To them, the value of any diskette is the same – full or empty – only a few dollars, or the value of the atoms."

He goes on to narrate another story when he visited the headquarters of one of the United States' top five integrated-circuit manufacturers. He was asked to sign in the visitors' register and, in the process, was asked whether he had a laptop with him. Of course, he did. The receptionist asked for the model, serial number and the computer's value. "Roughly US$1 to $2 million," the professor said.

"Oh, that cannot be, sir," she replied. "What do you mean? Let me see it."

He showed her his old PowerBook (whose PowerPlate made it an impressive four inches thick), and she estimated its value at $2,000. She wrote down that amount and he was allowed to enter. The world of atoms would soon become a world of bits; the value of the intellectual property was being understood, appreciated and respected. Today, we see how quickly a pandemic induced digital transformation is sweeping across the world. We are collaborating communication, co-creating over digital platforms as we work from home. The atoms have become bits in a few months.

Uncomfortable about being too comfortable

My life was about to be transformed, and here I was standing on the edge of chaos. Our well-settled lives in the US of A had lulled us into a sense of comfortable existence, especially for us from India, who had faced daily struggles in our middle-class lives of commuting in crowded transportation, over-potholed roads, suffering the scarcity of resources and lack of jobs. Somehow, I always felt uncomfortable with being too comfortable. A challenge-free life looked dull and uninteresting. It wasn't as if I was seeking trouble, but the mind needed a fresh problem to solve, a mystery to unravel, to find answers to questions given up by others.

The MIT professor almost grabbed me by the lapels of my jacket and shook me up when he spoke about an information highway. The six-lane highway in which I drove my car was no longer seductive enough for me when I looked at the vision of the digital highway he painted before us. "The information superhighway is about the global movement of weightless bits at the speed of light. As one industry after another looks at itself in the mirror and asks about its future in a digital world, that future is driven almost 100 percent by the ability of that company's product or services to be rendered in digital form", he wrote in his book *Being Digital*. Jobs, he said, would flow through telephone lines across the world to where talent was available.

If that was going to be the case, then soon, the things I knew as atoms could be transformed into bits. Music, movies and books didn't need to be atoms. My mind went crazy thinking about things that were atoms that could soon be bits. I looked at my work; the programs we were writing in our PCs or laptops, the projects we were managing suddenly appeared to be moving around chaotically as zeros and ones, yet there was a method, a pattern, in this maddening swirl.

The information superhighways, the MIT professor spoke about, were not constricted by physical boundaries. These could cross oceans, mountains, borders, travel seamlessly through countries and continents. If we had connectivity, any place in the world could be our workstation. My imagination was working overtime as I went through the professor's words "bitcasting" via optical fiber cables and satellites, digital television, computer graphics, computer-generated music and computer-enhanced learning.

Geography was history

I kept on analyzing my work and thinking of his remarks about the increasing globalization of work into a seamless, digital whole with software constructed by moving work-in-progress around the digital medium to coincide with international time zones. Where people are released from the limitation of geography as the basis for friendship, collaboration and 'neighborhood' and where each new generation becomes more digital than the last. For the first time in my life, I started realizing that geography was rapidly becoming history.

Nothing, I reasoned, could stop this tide of disruption sweeping over us. The choice was to pick the best place to ride this surf or be overwhelmed by it. Back home in India, things were beginning to change, software exports had just crossed the billion-dollar mark in 1996-97 and were growing at a fair clip of 50%. According to India's Ministry of Information Technology, the software industry was projected to export $6 billion worth of software by 2001, and it hoped to reach a then-jaw-dropping figure of $10 billion by 2002.

Indian software was expected to be a $5.7 billion industry in 1999–2000. In December 1999, a National Association of Software and Service Companies (NASSCOM) – an organization representing the Indian information technology industry – report forecasted that by the year 2008, software and services would contribute more than 7.5% of India's overall gross domestic product growth with IT exports accounting for 35% of the country's total exports.

The watershed year of this revolution was 1998. Indian companies, like Infosys, Satyam Infoway (later Sify) and TCS, emerged as world players as fears loomed over computer problems expected to erupt on January 1, 2000, famously known as the Y2K Bug in those days, and preparations for the European Union's new currency unit, the euro. These drove demand for Indian software programmers. American companies, such as Texas Instruments, Microsoft, IBM, Oracle, Motorola and GE Capital, established operations in India, including software-development centers.

Disruption as usual

There was a buzz in India, and I wanted to be where the action was. The technology industry is not insulated from the big political, social and economic currents, and it was important to understand and take advantage of the interplay of these dynamic forces. Every time I heard phrases like 'big shifts are taking place', 'the future of work is changing', 'organizational transformation is critical', 'digital transformation' or 'disruption', I can't help feeling a sense of déjà-vu. I am getting the same feeling today as the world grapples with the impact of the COVID-19 pandemic.

Disruptions have always been there and will be there. In fact, it is business as usual or disruption as usual. What has changed now is the velocity of this disruption. Change or transformation is coming at us at an incredible speed and my favorite quote has been: "Change will never be as slow as it is today."

The limitless capabilities of the human mind can only be discovered when this amazing thing called disruption hits us. Whenever challenged with adversity, humans invariably summon the tenacity and diligence to fight the odds. I find chaos highly exhilarating, like a surfer who travels around the world seeking the biggest, most fearful and extremely daunting waves to ride on. Let's face it, the world is actually a very chaotic place. Just under the calm surface of the Earth, the core of the planet is a burning cauldron with molten metal swirling in temperatures ranging from 4500-degrees-centigrade to 6000 degrees centigrade.

The oceans around us are in constant motion, with violent storms forming every day as its surface heats up from the sun. The space beyond our atmosphere is a violent place with asteroids or meteoroids hurtling at breath-taking speeds toward the Earth and missing us every moment. Life itself is a precarious exchange, so why be afraid of chaos? We human beings are custom created to survive disruption and chaos through our creativity, innovation and indomitable spirit and keep turning obstacles into opportunities.

The rate of disruption, change or transformation is hitting us at an incredible pace across every industry, thanks to an increase in computing power, technology adoption and information sharing. Markets have become more efficient due to these global shifts. Moreover, companies have gained access to a broader pool of talent and resources, allowing them to challenge global competition. The resulting changes and pressures are challenging virtually all companies, from start-ups to established enterprises.

Goliaths dancing the Davids

Disruption is not just a matter of 'technology-first' companies uprooting legacy competitors. Even recognized veteran players, who had capably adapted to technology, are also making new moves to gain market share. In the face of rapid change, many companies are feeling uncertain about the future. Leaders, at times, are nervous.

It's happening because of two major misreadings of the situation. We think that disruption happens by chance, rather than resulting from predictable forces, and that the only possibility is a winner-take-all situation. Typically, neither of these scenarios is the reality. Disruption can be positive for an industry, forcing legacy players to inject a new level of innovation and continue to evolve, while start-ups bring new ideas to the table. And when larger companies collaborate with smaller companies, they can generate new ways of thinking that benefit their customers and the industry – an ecosystem is created. In this new world, we will see collaboration as the key to success. We will see Goliaths dancing the Davids.

In some cases, a new technology-driven business model can completely disrupt incumbents (think Blockbuster in the face of streaming video services). I recall our childhood days in school when, at times, we skipped classes to watch a new Bollywood film first day, first show. The poster at the movie theater announced, "Now Showing." The other day, when I was driving down to the office, I noticed a huge billboard from Netflix saying, "Now Streaming." This was a digital transformation in one mighty sweep! An entire bank was on my smartphone; the world's hotels were just a click away as were the restaurants in my town. I can be at home, yet enjoy the finest cuisines available in the city. The world's best teachers were a click away. Let's face it: Everything that can be digitized will be digitized. Physical products are coming embedded with sensors that are constantly transmitting information, creating the age of cyber-physical devices. We are witnessing the foundations of the Fourth Industrial Revolution.

The car stereo played 'Take me home'

Change is always scary or daunting, but it doesn't have to be that way. Companies that efficiently adopt new technologies and adapt to new ways of working can survive and thrive amidst disruption and emerge as industry leaders. The threat of competition provides an opportunity for legacy companies to become more innovative, which ultimately serves consumers and strengthens the playing field.

It was also in this context of continuous turbulence that I decided to write this book – when tectonic shifts are changing the technological landscape, impacting economies, organizations and individuals. It is important to understand these shifts, quite a few of which I have personally encountered, having been a part of those and taken advantage of such transformations to grow and at times even fail.

The next few chapters will be my attempt to share some of the most important lessons I have learned; lessons that are universal and will remain constant regardless of the changes around us; lessons that will help us to stay relevant amidst the chaos. Some of these learnings have little to do with technology or transformation but has everything to do with rediscovering ourselves and finding out the art of staying relevant in a turbulent world. As I re-read the chapters before sending it to the publisher, I was surprised at how true these lessons have remained even today when the pandemic is unsettling our lives and livelihoods. I feel fortunate to have been able to experience these transformations and pick up invaluable lessons.

Way back in 1998, as I drove back from the grocery store one day, the radio in the car started playing John Denver's *Country Roads Take Me Home*. Denver is one of my favorite singers. The next thing I remembered was sitting on a British Airways flight, a tad scared at forsaking my established career in the Valley and leaving behind the country of milk and honey.

Chapter 3

Life Isn't Fair, but You Don't Have to be Unfair

As the British Airways flight from the US touched down at the Netaji Subhas Chandra Bose Airport in Kolkata, I could sense the unease of my children, in sharp contrast to my excitement about soon seeing my parents, sister and friends, some of whom had come to receive us at the airport. The airport then was a far cry from the smart, clean facilities that one sees now. It was chaotic, crowded, loud and confusing.

Life wasn't fair for my family, especially for my children. My daughter was too little to understand things and form an opinion, but my young son, barely five years old, suffered his first culture shock when we were piling into an old Ambassador car as we got out of the airport.

"This isn't our car!" he wailed and simply refused to get into it.

In his mind, cars were supposed to be shiny, sleek and handsome. That's what he took as normal in his young life spent mostly in the US and, for a while, in Europe. The contraption in front of him dealt a devastating blow to whatever little expectation he had of me in a new land.

The next shock was when he saw a driver behind the wheels, who wasn't his father. "Daddy has to drive!" he screamed. He didn't have confidence in someone else at the helm. Everything here was disruptive for him. His life was being turned upside down and he had no control over the situation. It was like being hit by a series of events, each one more shocking than the last.

In school, he didn't understand the language his new friends spoke. After his first day at school here, I asked him how his day was. He replied, saying everything was fine but at times, the other kids spoke a language he could not follow.

"I guess it was Dutch," he concluded, looking grim.

I suppressed my laughter and patted his back.

Everything was Dutch

I had indeed worked on a project in Amsterdam for about a year before returning to India. So my son went to his first preschool in the Netherlands, and it was Dutch, besides English, that everyone spoke there. Dutch was a language he didn't understand. Back in India, they were speaking Hindi at school, and it was a language he could not understand. Hence, it had to be Dutch.

On the other hand, I was in control of my life in India. I was back where the action was. My decision at that point in time seemed like a cruel one, thrust by an unreasonable father on his little ones. A few months ago, they were happy in a modern, developed country and now they were in an unfamiliar situation, hating every moment of it. But life's like that. As the saying goes: "It takes just a moment for things to change". It has happened to me so many times that happiness, joy and disappointment seem to blend into each other, leaving me unaffected. Maybe I was giving my children a lesson in life, which was a weak justification to myself.

Years later, they are happy in their respective lives, and I am a happy man as well. But I am a happy man who always thinks of what could go wrong, of how our lives could be turned upside down in one moment. Sounds contradictory? Perhaps it is. You could ask how thinking about why things wouldn't work could make one happy. Well, this is something life taught me one bitingly cold afternoon in a strange US city, St Louis, Mississippi. I was trudging five kilometers through the snow with my wife, our hands burdened with plastic bags overflowing with grocery, their weight cutting through our numb fingers. The bags were heavy as we couldn't make the trip twice a week so we loaded as many supplies as we could. I didn't own a car then, so the weekly five-kilometer trek was our only option.

That very moment, it struck me like a lightning bolt that life isn't what I, as a young man, imagined it would be – fair and rewarding for anyone willing to work hard and honestly, with sincerity and intelligence. Life wasn't fair. It was an incredible thought for a person like me, who had grown up in an ordinary middle-class Indian family, being mentored unspoken by hardworking parents about the eventual rewards of simplicity, hard work and honesty.

My father was a defense personnel who worked on technologies that supported information systems security in the Indian Air Force, and my mother was a junior central government employee. She attributed all our achievements to the will of the almighty, like any Indian mother. In fact, it was my father who had suggested, way back in the seventies, that I should learn things about computing, which one day was going to become an exciting new opportunity. He was one of the first people I knew who used computers.

Hardship was life as usual

My realization about the unfairness of life didn't have anything to do with lugging a heavy grocery bag. In my childhood days, we were used to standing in a queue at a ration shop and coming back home with gunny bags full of grains, sugar and other necessities. Hardship in life was common when we grew up in a pre-liberalized India that was struggling through economic challenges. Like everyone else in our neighborhood, we faced the same trials. We actually took it as part of life and never thought of it as a hardship. This was life as usual!

Regardless of tough times, what didn't change was the belief that if you worked hard, you would be successful in the end. But it was on that icy winter afternoon, with the harsh wind cutting through our jackets, that I realized it wasn't just hard work or honesty that mattered. What mattered most was being aware of the ecosystem in which you worked and managing this environment, so that your contribution was not ignored by the leadership and received its due recognition.

One need not have to change one's own belief in fairness. One only needed to accept the fact that not everyone around you would be fair and take that into consideration. You needed to understand and accept the fact that the world will not always follow your playbook.

From being naïve to being aware of the ecosystem's in-built biases was the realization that dawned on me that day. It's like being a good driver, playing by all the traffic rules and at the same time, constantly on the lookout for bad drivers who didn't know how to drive, simply ignored the road signs or wanted to edge past you fairly or unfairly. Sometimes, they knew the rules but interpreted it in their own way to their advantage. It happens all the time, even today. A good driver just keeps an eye out for these people and knows when and how to avoid being hit and stay on course to reach the destination.

On the verge of losing my job

While in the US, at one point in time, I was nearly on the verge of losing my job and didn't have the money to fly back home to India. Barely managing to live on survival wages, which meant living in a tiny room with my wife above an Exxon Mobil gas station and sleeping and eating on the carpet, I figured out that I had to make life fair for me and my family. I called my home office back in India, asking for help. In response, they sent a colleague over to my tiny room above the gas station to validate how I lived and check out whether I was making needless fuss.

He didn't disclose this to me then but spent the night sleeping on the carpet with me. He reached my home on a Friday evening and then took my wife and myself out in his car on a trip to Chicago over the weekend. We had a princely lunch at McDonald's because that's what we could afford. It was my first trip out of the apartment in the three months since we had come to the US, perhaps the only few moments I would like to remember from those days.

Nothing changed in my life since his visit, although he did communicate to our leadership team the difficulties I was going through, trying to make ends meet. But nothing happened. Nothing changed and no additional financial help came. The company was happy with its pie of the money coming from the 'body shopped' employee. It was too risky to raise it with the client and renegotiate the deal. Looking back after all these years, I can say that those were the days I learned how to take rejection, success, appreciation and criticism with equal grace and dignity and, at the same time, a stoic approach that everything, including good or even bad times, was transient. That was the biggest learning of life's lessons for me. Gracefully accepting things that I couldn't change and courageously trying to improve things that were within my power to do so.

I wasn't going down a quitter

Facing a terrible financial situation and a poor performance rating from an unreasonable supervisor, who was more of a boss than a leader, I had typed out my resignation letter and it was in my pocket when I reached the office back in India. It was strange that though my clients were rather pleased with my work, my boss wasn't. Then the thought hit me that if I quit that day, everyone would say that I was a loser and that I had poor performance and got a low rating, so I resigned. It was an eye-opener, a realization and a promise to myself that I wasn't going down as a quitter and that was final.

It wasn't how I wanted the story to end. I was too much of a plucky young man to give up before making one final thrust to turn things around. This was a time when one looked within to dig out the last scraps of energy inside you to lunge forward for one final dash toward the victory line. I had to script my own story in my way! I was like a boxer on the mat, put there unfairly, and could hear the referee count. At the same time, I could visualize myself holding my arms aloft in a winner's triumph. I had to turn this visual imagery into reality.

The year was 1975, the 1st of October, the football fans in Calcutta were in a frenzy that afternoon as Mohun Bagan, the legendary Indian football club, was facing its archrival, East Bengal, in the final match of the Indian Football Association (IFA) shield that season. Under the bars of the goal post was a rookie keeper, Bhaskar Ganguly. By half-time, Ganguly had spilled a couple of shots from the East Bengal strikers and a few brilliant moves had Bagan down 3-0. By the 51st minute, the scoreboard read 4-0 as East Bengal fans were euphoric. The goalie was replaced and by the time the match ended, it was a record-breaking 5-0 that devastated the club that had risen to fame in 1911, beating a British football team and triggering Bengal's love affair with football.

Everyone was certain that Bhaskar Ganguly's career was over even before it had begun. I had seen the match as a kid and didn't think about the Bagan goalie till the day I typed out my resignation letter. In a flashback, I was on the football field, watching a rookie goalie leave the turf with his head hung low, shoulders sagging – an image of utter dejection.

What happened thereafter was the stuff that legends are made of. For three months, Bhaskar didn't step out of his home. The next season, he switched teams and began an uphill journey marked by brilliant saves. Then one day, he became the nemesis of strikers coming to take a shot, and Ganguly under the bar. Three years later, he led India in the Asian Games in Delhi. Bhaskar Ganguly – the man who guarded the goal – was my hero for an incredible comeback.

I scripted my comeback story

I dug my heels and began to script my own comeback story in the next US project I was assigned to on my return. This time, it was in the heart of Silicon Valley, California. The weapons I could fight back with was grit, the ability to work harder than most and staying strongly focused on delivering delight to the customer. Only, this time around, I was aware of the biases in the system and individuals. One cannot fight those deep-seated traits; all one can do is to rise above these biases to doggedly excel in your work and take it to such a level that it is impossible to ignore you. I made myself virtually indispensable in the project so that taking me out would risk a drop in the quality of delivery and incur the displeasure of the customer, which my new manager couldn't afford.

From that day onwards, I never took things for granted and told myself that everything wouldn't be in place the way I wanted it to be. The biggest lesson for me was that I had to embrace the opinions of others without being judgmental about it. That's the day I realized the importance of seeing things from the other's point of view, which is what empathy is about. I tried to place myself in the shoes of my manager, who gave me the poorest rating possible, and attempted to understand his trigger points. His opposition was an opportunity for me.

The long hours I spent in the project office made it challenging for my co-workers, who felt pressurized and reacted negatively as they felt I was working harder to make them look less efficient. For me, it was not just a battle for survival. I had a point to prove. I realized the importance of achieving one's goals without hurting the sentiments of others. It was just that I drove like a man possessed yet abiding by the traffic rules and without crossing the path of others.

Prepared for disappointments

All the while, I was mentally prepared and toughened to deal with the unexpected disappointments that I was sure would come my way. There are certain things in life that are predictable and for which one can prepare, but there are unavoidable situations that will touch you eventually. There is an inevitability about it! This was what I learned. From getting battle-hardened to dealing with the next setback and preparing for the inevitable changes in our lives and business – it was as if I had rediscovered myself.

Disruptions and disappointments were business as usual but not regrets! Everything was a lesson learned and an invitation to come back stronger than ever before, building a formidable strength within to withstand and rebound with renewed energy. When the pandemic struck us, I delved deep into my reservoir of experiences and realized that this was a new kind of a challenge but certainly, nothing that couldn't be faced with the same weapons that had helped us survive and thrive before.

Later in life, it made me look differently at the organizations I worked for and had the good fortune of creating and leading and prepare them for disruptions, which were unavoidable and inevitable. Scanning the horizons for threats and opportunities, continuous learning, assimilating knowledge from clients, peers, colleagues, teammates and, most of all, competitors, helped me lead very large organizations through complex transformation journeys and emerge stronger, fitter and agile. In the same way, my personal stumbling blocks became stepping stones.

I did this by re-focusing my thinking and moving away from a languid mindset of expecting things to work out the way I wanted. I moved to the realms of understanding the unknown, trying to predict the inevitable and preparing for what was unavoidable. The neurons of my mind were electrified, trying to foresee what could go wrong and discovering unknown pathways to turn every situation into the next opportunity.

I was alert, aware and proactive. I was no longer merely reacting to situations but unconsciously determining the shape of situations. Bhaskar Ganguly once said in an interview that he could mentally influence the striker to shoot the ball in the zone he wanted to during a penalty shoot-out and that was the reason for his remarkable record of saving goals. He would stand a little more to his left or right, instinctively forcing the striker to aim for the side with a wider gap.

My learning to cope with adversity and the unexpected, later on, became a management tool in my arsenal. I found through personal experiences that you could either focus on the problem itself, trying to analyze the root of it and working harder to address it, or complain about it. You also needed an emotional response to the crisis or challenge facing you. This is about diving deep within yourself to bring out all the hidden energies to tackle the situation, instead of brooding, avoiding or denying the problem.

Focus on the things we can control, not on what we can't

The emotional response is useful when we cannot control or influence the problem we are facing. Instead, we can focus on what we can control – ourselves. This is exactly what I did. I trained myself to keep doing it with a fierce intensity. Sometimes in life, we all get bad bosses, projects that look destined to fail or relationships that sap our energies. I continually remember that life isn't always fair. The wrong guy seems to get promoted, and the evil person appears to be winning. It's time to work on ourselves, reimagine our strengths and transform ourselves. Life looks unfair when you aren't winning – that's the truth! So let's get our focus back to doing the job incredibly well so that winning becomes a natural by-product. Stop fretting about life being fair to the wrongdoers, and start focusing on upgrading yourself.

St Louis taught me to understand the importance of being fair and doing it with sincerity. Fairness resonates with your team, and even tough decisions made fairly will make people respect and appreciate you. In leadership roles, you'll have to make tough choices. Sometimes, it will hurt to do so, but if done fairly, it will reinforce your relationships and earn the trust of your team, friends and family. You don't always win by winning. The best outcome is everyone getting what they need.

The most important thing in life is not being the guy with the biggest car or the most expensive house. It is being the most trusted person. Trust, integrity and fairness will always have a premium, regardless of whatever disruption comes our way. These are essential skills to be learned and not merely character traits.

Much later in my life, the organization I was working for was facing strong headwinds – the competition was eating into our market share, the industry vertical we catered to was facing a downturn and the economy wasn't favorable. We had a tough choice before us to downsize and let go of people who helped build the organization, and some of them were there from day one.

As a leader, I had handpicked some of these people to join the organization. I called them in for a meeting and explained the situation. Then I offered them the most honorable thing I could do to save their jobs. I asked them if they would accept a pay-cut and ranks reduced by a few notches. The other option was to take a golden handshake and quit. All of them accepted lower salaries and ranks and stayed back in the organization. When things eventually improved, bonuses were handed out, which made up for the reduced salaries. All of them were happy. No one had to lose their jobs.

I looked at the people across the table as someone's father or mother, a husband, a son, a brother or a sister. I tried to think of how they would go back home to face their families without a job. This was the best I could do to save their jobs and, at the same time, help the organization cut costs. Some of us in the leadership team voluntarily gave up our bonuses and refused increments. Individuals had to be taken care of and larger corporate objectives also had to be achieved. It was a fine balancing act. Empathy and a sense of fairness became strategic management tools in this case.

Some layoffs are inevitable in a downturn. During the Great Recession, 2.1 million Americans were laid off in 2009 alone. However, according to a Harvard Business Review article, the companies that emerged from the crisis in the strongest shape relied less on layoffs to cut costs and leaned more on operational improvements.

Some Indian technology companies also followed the American example and had resorted to knee jerk layoffs. This severely tarnished their brand equity as stable employers. A year later, when things improved, those organizations were back in the hiring market. But by then, people were reluctant to join them. In some of these cases, layoffs proved costlier in the long run as they had to retrain the freshers they recruited.

Back in my US days, as I worked harder in Silicon Valley – now more mindful of others and aware of bad drivers – I realized that I was happier than before. My work had gradually become more impactful to the project and my relationship with the client got even better. I was really enjoying my work. Because of my performance and impact, my financial situation had improved. This time around, I was aware that I needed to ensure a decent life for me and my family. All just by working harder and making myself an important part of the setup. The resignation letter was still in my pocket.

Happiness at work became the solid fuel propellant of my work and that, I realized, was the secret sauce. It's easy for me to say now, but it was difficult then to find happiness when things weren't familiar. I just knew that I couldn't let others determine my future; it was in my hands as was my happiness.

Three winters had passed in the US. This time around in Silicon Valley, the work I had done was acclaimed within the organization. They created a marble plaque in our global training center in Philadelphia, which had the names of the five people who had gone above and beyond the regular call of duty and touched excellence. Mine was the fifth name on that list. My job in the US was done. It was time to return home. I handed over my resignation that day. I had scripted my own comeback story and that was just the beginning. I also understood that happiness was a choice. Being happy was my goal, not winning. I understood that failure happens when we put too much emphasis on winning instead of doing the job well.

Chapter 4

Walk a Mile in Someone Else's Shoes

As I looked at the marble plaque from my employer with my name on it – recognition carved in stone for my work – there was no elation in my mind, just quiet satisfaction of a job well done and letting my work speak for itself. I wasn't alone in that moment of fulfillment. My mind raced back to all those who had made it possible through their understanding and unspoken support. My family, those who had never complained of the hardship they went through and the grace with which they bore everything, and my colleague who had taken us out to McDonald's in St Louis on our way to Chicago. They were folks who had walked a mile with me in my shoes.

This was my friend, Anjan Mazumder. It was a small gesture for him, but to me and my wife, it meant a whole lot. Years later, when he told me that the real purpose of his visit was to check the veracity of my status and report back to the office in India, I was touched. During his brief stay with us, he made sure my dignity and self-respect weren't hurt in any way. At the same time, he communicated the support I needed from my managers back home. We create enduring friendships through this deep understanding of each other. To me, these are the most precious rewards of my career, which spans more than three decades – pearls of rock-solid relationships that have lasted years. In my own way, I always try to cement these relationships without any expectations.

Even today my day is made when I receive an unexpected mail from a colleague no longer working with me, recalling the days when we leaned on each other during difficult periods. No one can really put themselves in someone else's shoes and see things the way someone else does. But the effort to do so with all sincerity is what is required in our lives. This is not only to have healthy relationships in our personal lives but also to create new value propositions for the products and services we create.

Feeling what others feel

Unless we fathom the pain points of our clients, we would never be able to create a solution that will delight them. Understanding the expectations of the clients is a talent to be honed by all professionals. When a client representative briefs me on the work he or she expects from us, I try to think of how that individual is going to be impacted by what I deliver. It could be that their next career progression depended on the success of the project they were entrusting me with. As the pandemic halted our world, I tried to think how the lives of our colleagues, customers and everyone who depended on them would be turned upside down. To ensure that we were able to battle it out together became the motivation of my work today.

Without understanding what a colleague is going through in his personal life, we will never be able to figure out its impact on their work. There were times when colleagues needed sheltering from organizational upheavals that had put their jobs at stake. I have always tried to feel deep down how their lives would be unsettled if they went back home that day without a job. At times I have, to the best of my ability, tried to buffer them from such unfortunate events as I believed in their talent and goodness as human beings.

Most of the time, I was right as they later proved to be invaluable contributors to the organization's long-term success. We moved on in life. They found their own paths and I continued in mine. But we still stayed in touch. Their unexpected phone calls from distant lands in the middle of the night, recalling those days, is my reward, which is no less than the plaque I received in the early days of my career. These are unshakable bonds that were forged when we went through turbulent times together and stood by each other.

Looking at things from the other person's point of view really is the cornerstone of design thinking. Anything we create has a user, an audience or a buyer. Unless we understand how the product or service we created will be used by the client, we will never be able to design it. This feeling comes from compassion. For me, this has always been the driving force in establishing a strong relationship with the clients I worked for, my colleagues, bosses and the teams I had the good fortune of leading. It has helped me strike the most amazing relationships with the clients I served and their people. This has created a network that has survived our careers in the organizations that were the platforms that connected us in the first place.

This genuine understanding has also been the first building block of any relationship, even the not-so-good ones. I used it to try to figure out the issues my boss had with me. Once I could understand it, things became easier. From his point of view, the poor appraisal he was giving me was justified. I had to make it difficult for him to rationalize the rating with my quest for excellence, the feedback from my clients and colleagues. He could no longer overlook my sincere efforts and positive outcomes.

This was my way of responding to a situation that wasn't going my way. I had two options –argue and complain or fight back with renewed vigor to deliver excellent work. Finally, he relented because he was responsible for making the client happy for the organization, and I was the person delivering this delight. This time around, the organization couldn't take a chance of me leaving them, which would have been the case had they continued to rate me poorly.

Leadership is an attitude, not a routine

In life, we cannot choose our bosses, colleagues or the circumstances we face when we wake up in the morning. We will always be working with people we have never met before and the only way to create a healthy working relationship is by understanding what drives our colleagues and managers. In my experience of watching leaders who made a difference and as someone who led teams in different organizations, it is about human experiences, not processes. As Dr. Lance Secretan, the Canadian author best known for his work on leadership theory and how to inspire teams, so rightly said: "Leadership is not a formula or a program. It is a human activity that comes from the heart and considers the hearts of others. It is an attitude, not a routine."

Years later, a colleague of mine approached me with a poignant request. She wanted to work from home for a long period to take care of her daughter, who was suffering from a life-threatening illness. The processes of the organization didn't permit it, and she had explored every other possibility, but there were roadblocks everywhere. When she reached me with her request, I took a conscious call. Her child was more important than any process. I chose to look the other way and let her work from home and take care of her daughter. A couple of years later, I learned that the daughter was cured and pursuing her studies. This was also a job well done in my book!

Genuine compassion, for me, has been the bedrock of building relationships with friends, colleagues and clients alike. My career has seen tectonic technological transformations, but the one thing that has helped me ride every trend is my firm faith in relationships. I could gather teams with the talents necessary to design and create organizations that have gone on to achieve global acclaim.

The value is in compassion

Once we realize that compassion creates a unique value proposition, the question arises on how to weave it into our relationships, leadership or team roles and product or service design. If it is such an intense personal feeling, then how can one make someone else believe in it with equal sincerity? The only way I know is by showing them the outcome of empathetic behavior and how it creates the basis of design thinking.

The first step for me has always been listening with the objective of understanding the trigger points of the other person. Often, one must look for signals rather than exact words or phrases. I always scan faces while making a presentation to a client. If I find their faces brighten when I am trying to describe their problem, then I know that I have hit the right spot. I can see it in their eyes that they appreciate that I have understood their challenges correctly – that is more than half the battle won. The answers will follow if the problems have been correctly identified.

If you are listening carefully, the speaker will understand and respect you for it. In client situations, I find that those who have a grasp of both the technology as well as the business aspect of it, often have an advantage over others in understanding their issues. This kind of knowledge creates a platform for an integrated conversation with the design idea being the central piece, from which flows the product/service design, execution, production planning, sales, marketing and everything tied in neatly with the strategy.

The idea of empathetic conversation helps us avoid being judgmental, which otherwise could lead us to rush giving answers without listening properly. When you try to walk in someone else's shoes, the tendency of being critical will automatically disappear. Then you begin to resonate with others as they sense your interest in their challenges, lives and work. There have been several times during my interactions with clients that I could gain the deepest insights about how their organizations functioned or how they as individuals viewed the challenges facing them, just by listening carefully. Creating solutions to their business issues became so much easier when armed with insight.

Facing my own ignorance

There are two kinds of listening: one is passive listening and the other is interactive. I have used the interactive mode more often than being a passive listener. Asking the right questions during the discussions helped me to dive deeper into the causes of the situations they faced. It also helped me to ask myself the most challenging questions to unblock my existing mental model. I could come face-to-face with my own ignorance and appreciate the knowledge of the other person and enrich myself with it. One can never find an answer without acknowledging what you do not know.

I have developed this into a model for seeking solutions to the challenges of our enterprise. I gather a team and then place the problem before them. My inputs are limited to setting a sense of direction and not defining the outcome. The outcome emerges through a natural process of unfettered minds giving their best intellectual inputs without fear of being judged. For five consecutive years, the organization I now work for has been acclaimed as one of the best places to work. The feedback from the evaluating firm is that employees feel that we are an empathetic organization with one of the lowest attrition rates in the industry. It's a simple formula for both myself and the organization – listen, learn, lead!

Being compassionate in understanding a decision or trying to walk in the shoes of others when you are the victim of an unfair decision is not an easy thing to do when you are young. It took a lot of effort for me to understand an unfair appraisal. Even when I reached leadership levels, the system hasn't always been in my favor. There is a constant struggle to explain decisions, which look extremely logical and urgently needed when seen from the ground, whereas others fail to see your point.

At times, it needed hitting the pause button instead of trying harder to convince others about your ideas or position. At other times, one needs to step back from the action and introspect. *Maybe I'm not seeing the other point of view with as much clarity as I think?* Most of the time, we don't step back because we feel that it would be viewed as a defeat. My experience has taught me that regardless of how such a decision is perceived within the organization, it is often better to step back and let other ideas take over. Over a period, these ideas, if valid, will work out or fail.

A few years ago, Google analyzed the most valued qualities of its employees, and surprisingly enough, STEM (science-technology-engineering-mathematics) expertise came in dead last. The seven top characteristics of success at Google that emerged out of the study were all soft skills: being a good coach, communicating and listening well, possessing insights into others (including different values and points of view), having empathy toward and being supportive of one's colleagues, being a good critical thinker and problem solver and being able to make connections across complex ideas.

Organizations have found that authentic compassion is key to business success. Southwest Airlines of the US, which has been profitable for 45 years and continues to be so, has created an entire campaign titled *Every Seat Has A Story*. People fly for different reasons, from a medical emergency to a job interview or a vacation. Southwest launched a microsite to tell 175 unique stories of its passengers. This is behind the airline's transparency in setting its fare structure. The company is viewed as reliable and fair by fliers and is one of the key reasons for its continued profitability in an industry that has been extremely turbulent. If we have to focus on the frequent financial difficulties Southwest has encountered, we must also ponder on the fact that it is one airline that has clocked profits for 45 years in a row. Even during these COVID times, the airline is not cutting capacity as much as others in the business.

Dove, as a brand, tries to demonstrate empathy with its audience. Its *Real Beauty* campaign plugs into the idea that both women and men struggle with low self-esteem, and in turn, encourages empowerment and self-belief. The 'Real Beauty Sketches' ad that Dove ran in 2013 was based on customer insight, playing on the notion that just 4% of women considered themselves beautiful.

Dove hired a police forensic artist. His job was to create sketches of people without looking at them. He had to listen to the person describe themself. That was the first sketch. The second image of the person was created when someone else met them and described them. Inevitably, in all cases, the person in the second image was prettier than the image created when the individual described herself.

It was a hugely successful campaign and Dove did not even try to sell their products or bother to obliquely mention those. The campaign titled *You are more beautiful than you think* has become a landmark in advertising that is authentic and right from the heart. The ad elicited a powerful and emotional response in viewers, contributing to more than 20 million shares in the first week of release.

Being authentic

In the early days of my career, I was assigned a project in a Tata group company. I was responsible for the delivery. My organization, during the sales process, had promised certain timelines to the client. When I assessed the solution delivery, I realized that the promised milestones were not realistic. I clarified it with the client. My candidness was not appreciated either by the client or my organization. However, as I had forecast, we missed the deadlines and the project was in a crisis mode. The situation went berserk, and things were slipping out of our grip.

It was then that the client representative realized that I had indeed told him the truth about the schedules. We sat down and worked out a new plan that was doable. Not only was the project rescued and the client happy but I had gained the invaluable trust of the people on the other side of the table. I had faced such situations several times in my career and each time, I found that authenticity worked out in the end. I always put myself in the shoes of the client representative and tried to figure out how important the success of the project was to his or her career. My success was dependent on theirs. We had to walk in each other's shoes.

Chapter 5

Have Never Arrived: The Zone of Comfortable Discomfort

Walking in my own shoes and in that of others, I look back at the journey and discover how exciting it has been all the while, though it hasn't perhaps been comfortable for me except in short stints. However, I only realized that it was uncomfortable much later when I saw what comfort meant to most of us. Just think how much we waited for 2020 for exciting things to happen and when it did, it wasn't exactly what we wanted. The pandemic created a once-in-a-century turmoil in our lives. But I just sat back and thought, *Haven't I seen such chaos before?* Maybe not as severe and global, but certainly chaos has been a part of my life.

Our childhood was spent when India was a struggling underdeveloped economy where the scarcity of everything was part of life – food was rationed, as were a lot of other things. It took 18 years for a Bajaj Vespa scooter to be delivered. A landline connection took an average of five to eight years to be allotted by the government, unless one knew a Member of the Legislative Assembly or, better still, a Member of the Parliament. I remember the jubilation and celebration in the family when our black-

and-white television set, using a cathode ray technology manufactured by the government sector Electronics Corporation of India Ltd, was delivered almost after a couple of months it was booked and advance paid. Compared to this, a few months back, I bought a large-sized flat panel internet TV off the shelf.

I recall, in my childhood, we used to gather at a neighbor's place to watch grainy images, often interrupted by 'snowing', of a cricket test match being played. It was such an exciting time for us. None of us realized that these were hardships or irritants that shouldn't be there in the first place. Only now when households have three television sets in three rooms, and each of us watching our favorite programs alone do I realize the hardships of our childhood days. When we switch on the air conditioner at home or walk into a nice cool office today, I often think of the days when if power was available for half the day, we considered ourselves to be fortunate. We tailored our lives around when electricity would or wouldn't be there. I remember that the government used to publish a schedule of power cuts in the newspapers.

Apart from its disastrous anti-industry politics and aggressive trade unionism, West Bengal – sometime between 1978-85 – added a term as ubiquitous as *maachh* (fish) and *rosogolla* (sweet cottage cheese dumplings) to the Bengali vocabulary. 'Load shedding', a synonym for a power cut. Although for us school students, evening power cuts offered a welcome respite from homework. Surly adults irritated by the heat would force us to study by the light of kerosene lanterns. Candles were considered too expensive and always kept as a backup to be used only when the local government-subsidized ration shops ran out of kerosene.

At home, it was a daily chore to keep the kerosene lanterns clean and filled before dusk fell. In those days, we could swiftly reach for the matchbox and lantern even in the darkest of nights. It was a part of our survival skills.

The hot, humid, stuffy summers didn't bother us, youngsters, though. We simply lazed on the riverbank without shirts, cooling off in the breeze.

The freedom of my Royal Enfield Bullet

Coming to my job in Calcutta from our home in Barrackpore, in the northern fringes of the city, hanging outside an overcrowded bus didn't occur to me as something of a tough life. It was natural; everyone did it. So when I bought my first vehicle, a Royal Enfield Bullet motorcycle, with my earnings, the sense of achievement and liberation was boundless. It was an incredible feeling of elation riding the motorcycle all the 22 odd kilometers from home to office. I don't think it was the same when I bought a Mercedes later in life. It was wonderful being proud of working hard and seeing the results of it – a lesson that never left me. I looked for it in those who worked with me and felt inspired by them.

Life had prepared me and many like myself to take everything in stride. One was ready to go out to play the game regardless of the condition of the pitch or how tough the opponent was. The sense of life being tough never occurred to us growing up in those days of India trying to emerge out of third-world country status. We thought that this was how life was lived, and we had the responsibility to make it better. At the same time, we didn't think of ourselves as heroes, just ordinary youngsters trying to make it in a world where technology was promising to transform our lives. This was the time when one didn't have to be born rich. But armed with the right education, one could go out and win the world.

This was perhaps the best training ground one could ever have. Looking back now, I think it shaped the way I look at life, allowing me to see the trappings of modern life and never take anything for granted. There is a deep sense of appreciation of what life had given me, treating everything as precious, valuing those for their true worth and being confident that I could manage without them just as easily. This is the lesson of life that I have carried on to the organization that I work for – to take nothing for granted.

Optimistic about the future, realistic about the present

When the best of quarterly results come in, I can't find myself to be elated. Rather, I think that this is the time to invest in the future as the good times aren't going to be there forever. The technology that is giving us the advantage today will be disrupted tomorrow. Our clients will not be with us if we cannot constantly make them competitive and in the process, stay ahead of the curve ourselves. Likewise, when the graph declines in a few quarters, life doesn't look so dark either. It is just another challenge that needs to be battled out. It's like a sprinter pushing hard against the block, waiting for the starter's gun.

I am always optimistic about the future, a realist about the present and seldom overly romantic about the past. I think we have even more exciting things to come, but at the same time, we need to keep at it all the time so as to never let our guard down. To me, I have never arrived. The sense of having arrived will always be something alien to me. It is a feeling of being constantly on the edge, at the threshold of something even bigger and better about to take place. It is not just wishful thinking, but a realistic assessment of the transformations taking place around us and consciously elevating oneself to play an active part in it.

My experiences of growing up in a modest economic environment, with a middle-class upbringing, also gave me a sense of calm acceptance of certain things that couldn't be changed but needed to be taken advantage of if possible. I don't always look at the past with rose-tinted glasses. A power cut in the evening when you are preparing for the coming exams is a huge irritant. But one could hardly do anything about it except use the daylight hours as much as possible or get a battery to hook up an electric bulb.

Our experiences were the same in India, regardless of where we grew up. Sundar Pichai, the CEO of Google, remembers the droughts in Chennai so vividly that even today, he can't sleep without a bottle of water by the bedside. The first time he boarded an airplane was when he took the flight to the US for his studies. His family also never had a television set. For that matter, he wasn't alone. The vast majority of Indian families at that point in time didn't have a television set.

Turning our childhood experiences, anxieties, fears, hopes and jubilations into positivity has become a part of living life. Psychologists would perhaps have an answer to why a very large number of successful people have gone through childhoods that weren't easy. I think it prepares one to appreciate success a lot more and never be defeated by the setbacks. That which does not kill us makes us stronger! How will you ever appreciate the good you've got if you don't know how bad things can get?

Moving out of my comfort zone

Such people have far greater adaptability than perhaps others who have had easier lives. They are more likely to step out of their comfort zone and try something different. When I moved out of my almost 20 years of IT career into telecom, I knew very little about this industry and the technologies involved in it. It wasn't my comfort zone, but I could see the big picture that the world will be driven by connectivity and mobile communication.

I could also connect my known dot of IT to Telecom and understand that ICT (information, communication and technology) was a game changer. It was my optimism about the future that led me to it and the adaptability skills that helped me to leverage my knowledge of IT to create new value propositions. I also realized that IT – as we knew it then – had to be redesigned to meet the needs of the emerging trends, when people wanted ever-faster communication and an almost insatiable demand for speed and connectivity.

Our skills and competencies needed to pivot around for this massive transformation underway all around the world. Redefining our skills was the only way to stay relevant, and we weren't afraid to make mistakes in the way of gaining fresh knowledge and experimenting with new things. Inside us lurked a sense of childish curiosity to dive into the unknown, like the way we learned how to swim in the river Ganges in Barrackpore – by being thrown into it. The pressure to perform wasn't really there, which I think made us bold enough with a dash of audacity.

Back then, no one ever forced us to be perfect in everything. As children, we were never under a burden to perform, be the best in our classes or be the highest scorer in all subjects. It was okay if we were good enough and tried our best. That was acceptable. Microsoft CEO Satya Nadella's father couldn't believe the poor grades his son was bringing home.

However, instead of pushing his son hard, his father said that Satya must be good at something else. His heart was in cricket, but he realized that he wouldn't be making a career in the game. He even failed to get admission into IIT. A faint spark of interest in computers made his father buy him a Sinclair ZX80, an affordable home computer launched by the British firm, Sinclair Research, in 1980. That became a passion and eventually took him to the University of Wisconsin at Milwaukee to earn his master's in computer science.

In hindsight, I realize certain things happened because of this lack of huge weight of expectation on us. We were never afraid of failure or tried to achieve the impossible task of being flawless. I became an 'audacious-realist', audacious enough to attempt what looked impossible and realistic enough to know that perfection was a continuous journey. It devastates me to read about children committing suicide because they could not get into tier-one academic institutes or do well once they got in. Even in school, we see this happening as children are unable to cope with peer and parental pressure.

Being audacious

In our careers too, we face projects that look daunting and chances of success are dim. My experiences of early childhood have built in me a risk-taking ability that goes beyond my skills. This comes from a feeling that things can't be worse than what they are, and if at all, it would be better. Someone could describe this also as being audacious. Audacity comes from the mental agility to adapt, accept and be analytical, which will be the most sought-after combination of skills in a world that will see more changes in the next 20 years than what we have witnessed in the last 200 years.

My way of looking at it was optimizing my own performance by attempting things that others considered difficult and seeking the thrill of achieving it. However, it wasn't as if I hadn't weighed the risks of the assignment. If it passed my test of 70 percent possibility of success, I would go for it. We learned to step out of our zone of comfort with a sense of adventure.

Richard Charles Nicholas Branson had dyslexia and poor academic performance. On his last day at school, his headmaster, Robert Drayson, told him he would either end up in prison or become a millionaire. Branson, according to some, inherited his business DNA from his entrepreneurial mother, who was successful in building and selling wooden tissue boxes and wastepaper bins. Despite early unsuccessful attempts to grow and sell Christmas trees, Richard's first rewarding venture was a magazine named Student, launched in 1968. A year later, his net worth stood at £50,000. He was just 17. Thereafter, he sold records and advertised those through his magazine. It became an overnight success.

Since then, Branson has made a habit of moving out of his comfort zone. That has become the secret sauce of his continued success, besides the uncanny ability to spot opportunities where there are obstacles. In 1984, Richard was trying to take a flight from Puerto Rico to British Virgin Island to meet his girlfriend, Jane, who he later married. The flight was canceled as it didn't have enough passengers. Most of us would have looked for a hotel to spend the night or try to take another flight. Branson didn't have money to charter a flight but thought it was a good idea to reach his destination. So he took a blackboard and wrote "$39 One-Way Flight" and chalked *Virgin Airlines* on the top. Then he rounded up all the passengers who had been bumped off and they chartered a flight and an airline was born, though he didn't know anything of the business. He's now working on space tourism and satellite launch business, once again far away from his comfort zone.

Failure, though, is nothing new to Branson. His career graph is studded with a long string of unsuccessful entrepreneurial ventures. This includes Virgin Publishing, Virgin Cars, Virgin Cola, Virgin Clothing and Virgin Brides. And therein lies the strength of his never-say-die spirit. He dares to think different and beguilingly simple, even when things do not go as planned. Whenever an idea failed, he bounced back with another. As he wrote: "There's nothing wrong with making mistakes as long as you don't make the same ones over and over again."

The current pandemic has thrown tough challenges at Virgin Atlantic as it has to all other airlines the world over. Reports indicate that Branson is putting up the luxury Necker Island he owns as collateral for a commercial loan to save the airline. There are also talks of a major sell-off of shares in his space venture, Virgin Galactic, to help the group tide over the COVID crisis. But people who know Branson are confident that the maverick entrepreneur, so used to risk-taking, will surely bounce back yet again.

Branson summed up his attitude beautifully when he said, "If you opt for a safe life, you will never know what it's like to win."

Schools don't teach us to collaborate

It is this false sense of safety that has perhaps become the biggest roadblock to innovation in the IT industry in India. Those who have been meritorious enough to have gone to the best engineering and management institutes have developed a sense of entitlement. More often than not, they would have had a fairly easy life focused on being the best, looked after by parents who tried to meet their every need. Of course, they were far more academically brilliant than most of us. Their achievements are what make us proud of them.

Experience has shown me that there is often little correlation between academic brilliance and success in our work environment. Being very good in studies in school and college is about an individual's intelligence, dedication and hard work. While in the workplace, we need to be good at teamwork and collaboration, something that is rarely taught in academic institutions. There is a large degree of dependency on others also performing their roles well if one is to be successful in our professional lives. This is not the case when one is preparing for their exams in college. In one's sheltered academic career, one has loads of competitions. But these pale in comparison to the harsh realities of the practical world.

The parents of these academically successful people, at times, came from the same socio-economic milieu that I did. They grew up in a different India when things were scarce, and now, they want to give their children a better life than what they had experienced. There is nothing wrong with it, but does it create a sense of having arrived when these privileged young people begin their careers? Does it take away from the adventurism? Does it make them wilt under the slightest hint of tough times? Most importantly, does it fail to teach empathy?

One of the biggest and perhaps the most important lessons of my childhood was learning to be compassionate, without ever being told what it is. It was natural to nurse the swollen ankles of a friend that were twisted in a football match played barefoot. It was normal to share things, to huddle around the black-and-white television set to watch a cricket test match or listen to the transistor to the running commentary of a hockey match between India and Pakistan.

Today, there is a sense of loneliness in our existence of having television sets in every room. It is the paradox of 'having arrived', being able to afford multiple cars, large apartments and gadgets. Our sense of sharing that created the feeling of empathy is fading away fast. The more we put on our earphones and listen to music alone, the more we cocoon ourselves, losing touch with others. The more connected we are with the rest of the world, the more disconnected we become from those near us, and therein lies the challenge of losing out on empathy, the cornerstone of leadership.

I have always tried to fathom what is driving the other person. Whether it is a client or a colleague, in every discussion I try to figure out this key question and once I have the answer, things fall into place. If I understand the motivation behind an individual's action or inaction, then it is easy to resolve differences or arrive at win-win conclusions and is a pathway to successful negotiations. This feeling of empathy will be in greater demand in the future as our problems become more complex in these disruptive times.

Today is not the day of the risk-averse

You can't navigate your company or yourself through continuous change if you are constantly seeking safety and are risk-averse. To find new opportunities – and threats – in this fast-changing environment, we must learn how to be comfortable with uncertainty and chaos. And by that expression, I mean learning how to stay calm while poised at the edge of uncertainty, remaining ever attentive to elusive clues both in our surroundings and in the way we perceive the moment of crisis. You are always at the edge, never arrived, never settled but intensely comfortable with chaos.

We're living in an age of accelerated disruption that will upset our existing business models and our lives. Those who have the front-row seats in this unprecedented transformation are often too involved in the technological aspects of it, forgetting the human side of things. Little attention has been paid to the cognitive and emotional load that any change of such magnitude creates for the individuals involved. In this COVID-normal world, we do not know what awaits us tomorrow. The pandemic is coming in waves. Just when things look like they're under control, another spike in the number of cases hits us. Lockdown is not followed by an opening up but by another lockdown. It is becoming useless to plan long term. We need to accept the realities and create agile planning for short-term goals.

Our management or technical education does not prepare us well enough to handle these kinds of scenarios where goalposts are constantly changing. Every industrial revolution has caused pain and it will be no different now. The world is battling three crises at the same time – a pandemic, an economic recession and geopolitical tensions where globalization is being replaced by localization. At the same time, a flurry of technologies is being unleashed to help us continue our economic activities in a contactless world.

I have always believed that unless technologies make our lives better, we have lost the purpose of it. It is not a utopian thought, but concern about the planet, people and traditional economies will actually create exciting new business models. It will teach us that successful business models should be centered on achieving sustainable economic goals. Faced with pandemic and climate change, society is demanding that companies, both public and private, serve a social purpose. As BlackRock CEO, Larry Fink, puts it succinctly: "To prosper over time, every company must not only deliver financial performance but also show how it makes a positive contribution to society."

The ability to genuinely understand the emotions of others by experiencing feelings with them or through them will lead to innovation.

Products like Kindle were designed out of a desire to bring a vast repository of knowledge to readers.

As an SAP consultant at the beginning of my career in a Big Four consulting firm, I built my success around an authentic desire to make the client successful. I took on every problem as my own and tried to resolve it by placing myself in the shoes of the person I was dealing with on the client's side. This resonated with my employers as well as with my client. It worked when I took on projects that were important to the organization's success, rather than my own. I couldn't be successful if the organization I worked for wasn't. This was my motivation; it was a rather subconscious feeling that energized me.

Gen Z enters the workforce

As I look forward and back at the same time, I notice a distinct change between generations, something that once again makes me optimistic about the future. I can now see that the new generation – Generation Z, those born between 1996-2000 – will be entering the workforce differently from their predecessors – the millennials – who were exposed to an avalanche of technologies. Generation Z has always known the internet. They have always been connected. They were born in a world with smartphones.

Gen Z are the future employees and consumers. They will make up the largest portion of the workforce and are worth $1 trillion in consumer spending. They don't just work for a paycheck; they want a purpose. For them, work must have meaning. They want to work for organizations with a mission and purpose. If a company wants Gen Z to buy its product, this consumer group needs to buy into their brand story first. This story must be woven into a sustainable business strategy and backed up by data. Sustainability is not a cost but makes for a strong business case.

There are two strong push factors for businesses to adopt sustainable models of operations. The first is to manage risks arising from climate change such as disruption of operations and supply chains from extreme weather. The second is the strict regulatory environment adopted by most governments, increasing the cost of compliance.

It is humbling to note that compared to the millennials, Gen Z is far more socially conscious. They are keenly aware of climate change, look for authentic leadership, understand the concept of lifelong learning and, most importantly, are open and adaptable to change and trying out new things. I seem to resonate easily with this Gen Z, who take chaos, disruption and transformation as business as usual. They are, in many ways, like my generation, who were adventurous and, I think, a bit idealistic.

In many ways, those of us in our fifties realized that if ever that feeling of having arrived overtook our natural adventurousness, it would be the end of the road for us. Speaking for myself, I don't think I have arrived even today. The most thrilling and perhaps the most satisfying phase of the journey is about to begin.

Chapter 6

Gen Z: Post-COVID Tech Transformation on Steroids

Like any father, I was worried about my daughter, who's in college in the US, where the COVID-19 pandemic has hit particularly hard. She's self-isolating on her university campus. The other day, I called her up on video chat to find out how she's doing. Rather surprisingly, she's quite occupied and has created a busy schedule for herself, doing everything online from picking up new skills on YouTube to stay relevant to having Zoom parties with friends.

Curiosity led me to ask her about the apps she was using. She instantly created an Instagram poll, asking which app her friends preferred. A few hours later, Instagram emerged as the choice among her friends with Snapchat coming second. My son, in his mid-twenties, also wasn't complaining as much as I was. Honestly, I was getting a bit grumpy, unable to step out.

It struck me that Gen Z, to which my daughter belongs, is the first group in history that has never known a world without the internet. They were immersed in the online world since birth, Therefore, they weren't feeling as isolated as those of us in our early fifties or late forties.

Born digital

Gen Z, born between 1996 to 2000, are the first generation to view the digital and physical worlds as one. While they may still shop in a brick-and-mortar store, they use their phones to price, shop or seek out their friends' advice while doing so. For them, being digitally connected is an essential part of life. Perhaps the most important data is that Gen Z makes up 32% of the world's 7.7 billion population.

A McKinsey research echoed my conclusion that Gen Z-ers are digital natives. A third of them spend six hours or more a day on their phones. Gen Z also spends more time on social media than any other age cohort in Asia. They're more careful about how they use it: 36% of Generation Z respondents say they "carefully curate" their online presence. They are also more likely to follow their favorite brands and use social media and video-based platforms when making fashion decisions – as the McKinsey study revealed.

For Gen Z, life in a digital world is as natural as being in the physical world. They are the 'always on' generation. To them, the internet is an extension of their lives, a shared space for them to socialize, shop, entertain, seek information and devote a large portion of their time. For Gen Z, the distinction between 'online' and 'offline' is blurry, whereas other generations still have clear boundaries between both.

I could still recall that my initial attempts with Skype or Zoom were memorable for all the wrong reasons. I thought if I was on another window and couldn't see the person I was Skype-ing with, they couldn't see me either! Also, it was funny to see everyone staring at the camera and making faces, just to check which expression made them look better.

I am sure there will be plenty of research post-COVID-19 on how we adapted to this new way of life, but even without that, I can tell you that Gen Z haven't had to readjust themselves too much. When we think that remote work will become business as usual in a post-COVID-19 World, Gen Z are best suited to acclimatize themselves to this way of working.

The physical and digital world merges

As they step into a career in these COVID-ridden times, their professional lives are starting in the digital world straightaway. But it is nothing unusual for them; their digital personal lives are simply getting morphed into a professional one. They are being interviewed online through AI programs. Visual analytics are being used to profile them during the interview, and when selected, the process of onboarding the recruit is happening without physical touch. It's a completely digital experience.

In the post-COVID world, HR has created digital versions of the different forms that one had to fill up. Even banks have stepped up their game to open salary accounts and are issuing credit cards to create a start-to-finish touchless experience. Gen Z finds nothing unusual about this. It's just an extension of the online lives they were living before. "Touchless experience", another new jargon got added in our life.

A digital transformation of the entire process of selecting candidates to interviewing and onboarding has happened in a matter of weeks, which would otherwise have taken months or even years. In a survey of 11,000 workers and 6,500 business leaders by Harvard Business School and Boston Consulting Group, the vast majority said that employees' expectations for flexible autonomous work, better work-life balance and remote working were the issues most affecting their businesses now.

Gen Z candidates also carry out extensive research on various companies before an interview. They use online boards, as well as texting their network of extended friends, to learn not just about the work that they would be doing but also the culture of each organization. Then they watch videos posted by individual employees, take a VR tour of the office space and review job postings for their next role. They are always collaborating to evaluate prospective employers, like the way they depend on peer review of products before making a purchase decision.

The natural digital collaborators

Gen Z is used to collaborating online with their friends to get school project work done, so getting remote work distributed by a manager through Microsoft Teams platform is nothing unusual. Their Zoom party experience is getting seamlessly transformed into a professional teamwork platform to get work done.

As both Gen Z and millennials are 'social savvy', it's unsurprising that they have a greater affinity for multiplayer video games that incorporate social features. These games have morphed into social avenues, where they can hang out virtually with families and friends. This experience has created the ideal foundation for remote collaboration and working.

Remote working is perhaps the most natural thing for a digital-first generation. They are now turning this into a distinct advantage when they are starting on the job remotely. They have little hesitation in introducing themselves in remote team meetings and building a network, applying the same principles of engaging in multiplayer games across continents.

This generation is ideally suited to create the right kind of customer experience in a post-COVID-19-world where digital touchpoints will be more than physical ones. Customers' normal lives have hit a pause button and will continue to be like this for some years to come, at least till such time a vaccine is developed.

Overnight, demand patterns have shifted. Overall online penetration in China increased by 15%–20%, according to McKinsey. In Italy, e-commerce sales for consumer products rose by 81% in a single week, creating significant supply chain bottlenecks. Customers need digital, at-home and low-touch options.

The gurus of customer experience

Even after the coronavirus has subsided, digital-led experiences will continue its upward spike. Businesses that will proactively play on this and effectively improvise their delivery model to offer consumers a sense of security, definitely gaining an edge. Gen Z has known this experience all their lives. Their digital experience will be invaluable in designing new customer experiences.

It took my daughter less than an hour to do a survey on which apps were popular. Research reveals that traditional customer insights techniques, such as surveys, often have an 18 to 24 day lag between launch and results readout. At a time when conditions can change from hour to hour, that can be far too long to deliver a useful perspective.

Once again, the Digital Natives of Gen Z are in their elements to carry out instant surveys. This will become important for companies to pivot around quickly to meet changing customer needs. This will be the cornerstone of agile innovation. Frontline employees are a company's eyes and ears on the ground. Solicit and collect employee feedback: It will prove useful in gauging how customers are feeling and how daily interactions are changing.

The same principles can be used by organizations to listen to the voice of their employees, carry out sentiment analysis and create policy responses. Tools and technology now exist to rapidly collect and aggregate real-time ideas and feedback from employees.

Creating omnichannel experience

Analyzing how social interactions and connections shape the preferences of millennials and Gen Z can help companies determine which product, brand, advertising and marketing partnerships they need to meet these consumers' needs and expectations. By tracking and learning from feedback and reviews that younger consumers provide across multiple platforms, companies can select the device, app and content partnerships that will best provide differentiated and personalized user experiences.

These are areas where Gen Z have a native edge over any other demographic profile. The way organizations leverage Gen Z to their advantage to create new value propositions, products and services will be a crucial differentiator in deciding between the successes and failures in a post-COVID-19-world. As the online and offline worlds converge, consumers expect more than ever to consume products and services at any time and any place, so omnichannel marketing and sales must reach a new level. For consumers who are always and everywhere online, the online-offline boundary doesn't exist.

Marketers, thus, have an untapped opportunity to leverage Gen Z input as employees. If Gen Z is in your target, as employee or customer, it's essential to create a customer-centric culture that's empowered to prioritize improving the customer experience overall. How to get there? One possible way could be to let Gen Z take the lead, specifically on reducing employee effort. Customer Experience (CX) leaders at progressive companies seek to understand the strategic opportunities that connect employee effort and customer-centric cultures.

Accept, adapt and take advantage

The most important aspect of this generation is the open mindset they have when it comes to accepting new technologies, concepts and ideas. They have already accepted that the world will never be the same as before. They adapted to this new way of life and are making the best of the situation. Their mantra is to accept the change, adapt to it and turn it to your advantage. They are one-third of the world's population and if they are more comfortable with remote working, then I can see that the post-COVID-world is not going back to the normal we once knew.

We had entered a new world where atoms (the physical world) were merging seamlessly with bit (the digital world). Way back in 1994, Prof Nicholas Negroponte, the founder of MIT Labs, in his watershed book, *Being Digital*, first talked about how atoms were going to become bits. This was the digital transformation that he was speaking about. We can now see it happening at a blazing fast speed as distance dynamics become business as usual.

Chapter 7

A COVID-Normal Future – Accept, Adapt and Stay Agile

Some years ago, during a business trip, I suddenly bumped into a client on the aircraft when we were 30,000 feet above sea level. I was sure that it would be a frosty conversation as his emails had hinted that this would be the last piece of work we would be getting from his company as he was extremely unhappy with our deliverables. However, politeness won the day and we were soon chatting. I gently nudged the discussion toward the sensitive issue.

He was candid about his disappointment with us. It gave me the opportunity to clear the air and give him a fair assessment of what had gone wrong and how things could be put back together again. He listened intently and shook my hand warmly and said he was glad that we spoke and not exchanged icy emails. "You know, you could never email a handshake." He smiled and said that we would soon be working together again.

I thought about the incident during this pandemic chaos and wondered about shaking hands, something we won't be doing for a long time to come. Things have changed and we've got to live with it.

Uncomfortable truths

Let's face an uncomfortable fact: COVID-19 is here to stay for some years to come. The promise of a vaccine is at least three years away, according to experts, and even if it is launched, there's no guarantee that it will be 100% effective. Everyone's talking about herd immunity but that's unproven. It has been around four decades now since the outbreak of the HIV/AIDS epidemic and we still don't have an effective vaccine against the virus that has claimed the lives of approximately 32 million people till now and has affected 75 million people around the globe, according to WHO (World Health Organization).

The future, at least for the next three years, will be a COVID-normal world. Our lives will have to accept this reality; our businesses will need to adapt to this fact and shifting goalposts will be a regular feature, requiring us to be even more agile. Only organizational or societal culture will keep us anchored to our purpose in these tumultuous times.

It's not the first time that we are facing an uncertain future. It happened during the millennium bug when we didn't know how our IT systems would perform after that Y2K cut-off moment. The 2008 Financial Meltdown created unprecedented turmoil in the US that sent shockwaves around the world. The 9/11 terrorist strike in the World Trade Center set off global conflicts and transformed international relations at several levels. Technological challenges, economic recessions and geopolitical conflicts had templates that were used to soften the impacts. Millions of coders around the world worked overnight to fix the Y2K bug, central banks in the affected countries rushed to provide economic stimulus and conflicts were contained within geographic regions.

Three world wars at once

The COVID-19 pandemic is an entirely different crisis with almost no parallel in the past. It is difficult to envision the future when we don't have analogies of the past. The world is facing three wars simultaneously: The pandemic, which is a health crisis of unprecedented proportions, a massive economic disruption and a geopolitical challenge when countries are decoupling from past trade relations, reversing globalization for more inward-looking policies.

The COVID-19 crisis is different from all past such disasters; it is coming in waves. Just when we think that the virus has stopped spreading, a spark appears in another area and soon starts spreading. It is challenging the best of healthcare infrastructure in the most advanced nations.

Trillions of dollars of fiscal stimulus have been announced by governments to rescue economies that have stalled as businesses around the world are shuttered. The International Monetary Fund has called this a crisis like no other. As per its forecasts, global growth is projected at –4.9 percent in 2020, 1.9 percentage points below the April 2020 World Economic Outlook (WEO) forecast.

The pandemic has accelerated structural change in the global economic system, but this does not come without consequences. As central banks offer trillions of dollars' worth in response packages and policies, this may inadvertently burden countries with even more debt. What makes matters worse is the threat of trade wars between major countries, which has the potential to destroy the gains of globalization achieved over the past few decades.

Within this given context, organizations and individuals must think about how to survive now and thrive in the future. I have always believed that it is futile to worry about what is not in our control; we cannot influence its trajectory. It is better to accept this as a fact and move on, focusing on things that are in our control. It took some of us a while to accept that the physical distancing and partial lockdowns will be a part of life, as it is the only way to stop the spread of the virus. Once we have accepted this reality, the task was to adapt to this truth and factor it in our next moves. These were tactical, the immediate and the strategic and long term.

In our offices, we immediately rearranged the layout to create physical distancing between those who had to report to the office for work. For others, we shifted to work from home. Connectivity, cybersecurity, collaboration platforms and communication protocols were quickly organized to enable people to work from home. Within months, we had pivoted to delivering remote work and productivity went up by a third in some cases.

Companies found that remote work also helped them rethink their traditional ways of working out of large office complexes or campuses. If employees worked from home, they didn't require those huge facilities. Rents and leases could be re-negotiated and big-ticket items like travel and logistics could be rationalized. In some cases, companies even gave up large swathes of their physical office spaces.

A digitally dexterous workforce

Remote work and reduced physical workspaces meant that organizations had to pivot around to launch their digital transformation, something which they have been postponing for a while. The transformation took the shape of a platform that connected the organization with its customers, partners, employees and, of course, its internet of things, which comprised the manufacturing or service delivering facilities.

This ecosystem, in turn, needs a digitally dexterous workforce to handle the platform and meet the requirements of a contactless economy driven by distance dynamics. To prepare for the COVID-normal future, large scale workforce transformation enabling employees with relevant skills in working with data has become an existential question. Organizations that will have a digitally dexterous workforce will survive and thrive, leaving others behind.

This workforce will be highly comfortable in working with data generated from the digital transformation. They will use data for decision-making. There are more people out there who use data to make business decisions than those who work with data. Researchers say there are one to two million data scientists and nearly five to ten million data and business analysts. But there are an estimated 50-65 million data workers who take business decisions based on data.

The decision-makers often use rudimentary tools like spreadsheets. A digitally transformed organization will adopt automated decision intelligence, which is targeted at this last but most important group of people with low data literacy but who wants to use data to drive decisions. There is a clear indication that automated decision intelligence will become a foundation of analytics for business decision-makers.

Automated Decision Intelligence

The heart of the automated decision intelligence process is to bring AI into the workflow as a primary processor of data. For repetitive decisions that only rely on structured data, we are better off entrusting decisions to AI that is less susceptible to human cognitive bias. Although humans are not a part of this workflow, we must understand that just automation cannot be the single-point goal of any AI-driven workflow. Sure, it may reduce costs, but that's only an incremental benefit. The value of AI is making better decisions than what humans alone can do. This creates step-change improvement in efficiency and enables new capabilities.

Removing humans from workflows that only involve the processing of structure data does not mean that humans are obsolete. A lot of business decisions depend on more than merely structured data. Vision statements, company strategies, corporate values and market dynamics are all instances of information that only exists in our minds and conveyed through culture and other forms of non-digital communication as well. This information is unreachable to AI but enormously germane to business decisions.

The key is that humans are not interfacing directly with data but rather with the possibilities produced by AI's processing of the data. Values, strategy and culture are our ways of reconciling our decisions with objective rationality. This is best done explicitly and fully informed. By leveraging both AI and humans, we can make better decisions than using either one alone.

For example, AI may empirically state the lower inventory levels in order to maximize profits. However, a company may opt for higher inventory levels in order to provide better customer experience, even at the expense of profits. In other cases, AI may determine that investing more money in marketing will have the highest ROI among the options available to the company. But a company may choose slower growth in order to uphold quality standards. The additional information available to humans in the form of strategy, values and surrounding market conditions can merit a departure from the clinical rationality of AI.

However, as we move toward AI-driven business, we must be careful that there are no historical data of an unprecedented disruption like COVID-19. This is becoming a challenge for organizations in building data models to forecast the future. It is terribly difficult for a retailer, for instance, to predict customer behavior since historical data models are most likely irrelevant now and no data currently exists to create new models. AI models also got confused with unpredictable human behavior, such as a maddening rush to stock up on toilet paper. The algorithms could make no sense of this. This scarcity of data is impacting analytics projects, especially when trying to predict what happens when lockdown measures are relaxed.

Organization culture as an anchor

If everything is so flexible and agile and goalposts continuously shifting, then it is most likely that people will be disoriented, unless they are naturally inclined toward living on the disruptive edge. For most employees, there is a need to stay solidly anchored as the forces of change swirl around them. It is the organization culture that will provide this anchor.

For instance, an organization culture that fosters innovation has by default institutionalized imagination as its DNA. Imagination is a critical element of scenario planning. How does one infuse employees with the organization culture when we are all working remotely? This is a critical question that most of us are grappling with. There are no clear answers as of now. Organization culture is all about the people one works with and feeling like a family that cares about each other.

After the initial excitement of freedom and flexibility that WFH brings with it, there will be a certain feeling of loneliness when working alone. Organizations will have to strike a balance between WFH and periodic meetings at the office. The use of technologies like virtual and augmented realities in the future will give us a feeling of being next to each other, but at the same time, we will long to shake hands.

Let me be frank, I am missing it. Let's hope that we will soon meet each other in flesh and blood. I am doing what I always do to bring people together – showing them that I trust them and that I have full confidence in their capabilities, demonstrating that I will do everything to make their remote life as comfortable and productive as possible and keep communicating with transparency.

The old school values of compassion, integrity, possessing a moral compass and, above all, doing the right things over doing things right will continue to be the guiding principles for all times to come and even in this volatile world. Above all, authentic behavior, whether it is from leadership or freshers joining the workforce, will be the most precious value that will sustain and create the organization culture. This authenticity will be like the air we breathe; we can't see it, yet we can feel it all the time.

Chapter 8

The Day of the Authentic Leader

To be honest, leadership was never an ambition for me; it never was part of my plan because I didn't have a plan. It just happened. I worked in every level of corporate designation in PricewaterhouseCoopers (PwC), a Big Four consulting firm, before I became a partner. Was that part of my career roadmap? No, it never was. My focus was always on doing the best job of whatever assignment I had with me without thinking of how it would add to my curriculum vitae.

Maybe my aspirations were limited by my humble academic qualifications, compared to my peers who came from the best engineering or management institutes from across the world. They perhaps felt that they were entitled to leadership roles. I, on the other hand, didn't harbor any such aspiration. Perhaps that is why my focus was on giving better than my best efforts for any job that I was asked to deliver. If it was successful, the next assignment followed and responsibilities grew in proportion. To me, every day was an exciting opportunity to prove myself, not only to the organization or the clients I served but to myself.

Leadership, to me, happened as a natural process without seeking it consciously as a career roadmap. When it did happen, I figured that I had the responsibility to build the careers of other people in my team and the organizations I eventually headed. I had to create leaders out of my teammates and let them flourish. That became my overriding task.

I kept on discovering what leaders were required to do as I went along my job. I found out that I had to be a shock-absorber, shielding my teams from different pulls and pressures of the organization. I had to do it to let them focus on getting a good job done instead of being distracted by the internal political dynamics of the organization. At the same time, I had to give them feedback on their work and gently nudge them toward the right track if things needed to be without micro-managing.

At IBM, and even in Ericsson, I realized that we were creating something new; something that hadn't been tried before in these organizations. It was natural that not everything would be ideal. There were cultural issues and challenges of the transformation of extremely large organizations that had centuries of rich legacy behind them. These were highly successful companies, and therein was their challenge: the curse of success! They had faced numerous crises in their lifetimes, spanning over 100 years, and overcame those to emerge successfully. However, this also meant that the leadership was tempted to apply the formulas that worked in the past to the new challenges, which were completely different from the ones they had faced earlier.

Most enterprises have standard responses to a business crisis. These would include headcount reduction, slashing costs such as R&D or training budgets. Very few organizations thought of doing things differently. Ericsson also faced business headwinds in 2017; however, their response was to increase investments in R&D. This helped the company to increase its strength in 5G technologies and created a competitive advantage for it. However, this is a rare instance of leadership with its sights on the long term, rather than tactical reaction for immediate results.

It was tough to make organizations understand that what got them here wouldn't get them there. All these issues needed careful handling without letting people feel the pressure. One of the biggest lessons I learned in those days is that people trusted authentic leaders.

Time to get authentic

Now is an incredibly good time for leadership that focuses on being authentic or genuinely trustworthy without trying – being sincere and true to who they are as individuals. Imagine walking into the office every day and being yourself. We have waited a long time for it, and now finally, the moment has arrived, driven by a new breed of socially aware employees, environment-conscious customers and technological transformations.

The need for authenticity across the board is supreme today as people look for trusted hands on the steering wheel when no other navigational instruments are working. The COVID-19 crisis is unprecedented in its magnitude of chaos when no proven responses are working. Every day creates a new challenge and a fresh answer. This is no time for the fainthearted. Only trust and transparency will work. These are the traits that young minds entering the workforce value the most. The new generation is looking for authentic teammates, leaders and organizations. These are true digital natives exposed to the internet, social networks and mobile systems. They are highly ethical in their behavior and seek to unveil the truth behind everything. They are least likely to accept anything just because it comes from the top but would need a strong 'why' to independently work out the 'how'.

They will apply their own lenses of judging all decisions by a set of moral values they treasure. We have already seen it in an organization where employees are forcing leadership to give up military projects or technologies that they deem harmful to humankind. On the other hand, they prefer their organizations to be more environmentally conscious and socially responsible.

As many CXO decision-making tasks become technology-assisted, leadership can now focus on being leaders in the truest sense of the term – those others want to follow and not be forced to follow because of hierarchy. This is the leadership in demand now; leadership that is empathetic, natural, genuine and, above all, creating other leaders rather than followers.

In one of my appraisal reports, my manager wrote, "You look beautiful from the bottom, but ugly from the top." He was right. To me, my loyalty was always to my people as I felt that it was the team that would deliver for the organization. My role was to shield them from the different pulls and pressures of the organization, which would distract them from accomplishing their tasks and disillusion them about the organization. As someone rightly said, people don't quit their job; they quit their boss!

As a manager, leader and team member, I have always believed that what is right for the people is ultimately right for the organization, and happy people translated into happier customers – that's the simple formula of a good business. This has led me to disagreements with leadership teams several times in my career, across different organizations. I have strongly opposed the desire to grow just to meet only the number targets. There has to be a greater purpose attached to these targets.

At times, I noticed that the leadership often got embroiled in turf wars, a legacy of the command-and-control mindset, fighting over who would control what parts of the business. Leadership battles were about who will control which share of the pie, rather than collaborating to increase the pie so that everyone had a larger share of it. Employees are the first to get a whiff of such ugly tussles in the upper layers of the management and lose faith in the leadership. The authenticity of leadership suffers in the process. If leaders are engaged in a turf war, their teams would soon follow on the same path, which will eventually hurt the organization.

Let's face it, no enterprise is free from the fallout of individuals competing with each other within the organization, rather than competing with the external forces. A leader's job is to keep the environment clean and let the team perform without such political pressures. Some of these pressures were created because of volatility and uncertainty one operated in. The old model of letting people compete among themselves and the best guy winning has to be replaced with a collaborative atmosphere with shared performance metrics, where all of us have to win for the team to win. That's the task of leadership to create this environment for people to excel and find their purpose.

Successful leaders were often judged by their ability to manage these unpredictable factors that sucked them into operational issues. Some of them enjoyed being in the thick of things and being highly regarded as effective crisis managers or troubleshooters. It gave them a sense of being in control of things. However, this command-and-control system is giving way to a new kind of leadership, where letting go of control is the key to being successful. It is leadership through empowerment. As more employees work from home, this old way of supervising work will become redundant. Empowered employees will work independently and will be evaluated by objectives. Monitoring will be replaced by mentoring.

Relinquishing control encourages subordinates and colleagues to thrive because as the leader renounces control, subordinates are empowered to show initiative. My biggest successes came about when I gave teams the 'why' and then let them figure out the 'how'. The command-and-control leader's approach is fine for improving operational efficiency. But today, we must supplement conservative approaches with more of the skills of the innovative leader. Leadership has been transformed from giving directions to inspiring others to achieve – that is the core of authentic leadership. This is what Gen Z would want from leadership.

The traditional tasks of leadership have become relatively easier in a data-driven decision-making environment. Today's organization, which has harnessed the powers of analytics, has given the corner-office the tools to take some of the most critical decisions with relative comfort. The availability of data and the analytic power to extract intelligence from it has removed many of the uncertainties and ambiguities that earlier leaders had to cope with.

A manufacturing organization, using analytics, can forecast with ~95% accuracy when its critical equipment would need replacement. Therefore, financial planning and budgeting can take place well in advance. No sudden breakdowns, as predictive maintenance takes care of it, so no operational crisis to battle in the event of an abrupt stoppage in production. The CEO of a fashion line has the tools that predict, with uncanny precision, the colors for next season, thereby creating a flawless supply chain. Financial institutions can have their investment decisions vetted or at times decided by near-perfect algorithms working out risk-return reports. Banks have Big Data to rely on to judge the creditworthiness of their customers.

While this will free up a lot of leadership time, it will also mean that leaders themselves must be on top of technology trends to guide the organization and be prepared for their own jobs to be transformed. This will be the new kind of skill that leaders need to learn to stay relevant. Making a conscious effort to staying relevant is the only thing that is in our control.

For a long time, management gurus have been struggling with finding a suitable alternative to command-and-control leadership. This was primarily because leaders were reluctant to change their behavior as they were paranoid that businesses would fall into chaos if the reins of control were loosened. The new age leaders will be the Chief Inspiration Officers.

Creating harmony for a new age

Twenty-first-century leadership has unique and new requirements that are very important to their organization's success. Now, we face ongoing debates on the issues of inclusion, fairness, social responsibility, the role of automation, the ethics of machine intelligence and how to lead in a networked society. These are concepts that were not considered integral to the leadership manifesto even a decade ago. Some of these issues were yet to emerge then!

This is the era of social enterprise, and financial results are no longer thought to be the only or primary measure of a successful business. Now, in addition to the bottom-line, organizations are judged on the impact they have on the social and physical environment as well as on their customers and the people who work for and with them. In such a climate, any leader who will only focus on cutting costs, improving margins and go all out in the marketplace to beat the competition, would be considered anachronistic and parochial. Such an outlook does not have a place in today's world and totally misses the newer challenges on the broader business horizon.

Leadership, I discovered, was something very similar to the job of a conductor in an orchestra. It is about creating harmony from the different instruments and musicians – all playing and looking at the same sheet of musical notes.

I remember a team member who was a very quiet person and believed in doing an excellent job but never drawing attention to himself. I noticed a threat that his career might not survive the organizational restructuring. The right thing to me was to retain him going against the tide of the organization and ensuring that he continued to deliver value. I tucked him away in a team to give him a safe zone to hunker down for the storm to blow over. Some time ago, one fine morning, I received a mail from him, telling me that he is now successfully leading a very important activity in the organization. It was a very polite thank you note that made my day.

My job has always been to find who is good at what and then create an environment for them to succeed as individuals and harness their unique talents for the benefit of the organization. The exciting part of the leader's job, which will never change, is this human touch of aligning the individual aspirations of a talented bunch of people with organizational objectives. It makes me happiest to see them succeed, and I know I will have a winning organization if I have people who look forward to their Mondays.

In the initial days of my career, I learned how to play the role of a team member contributing to the success and sharing the challenges of the teams I was a part of. I learned how to lead these teams and sometimes, I was leading my peers as well as juniors. It was important to respect each member of the team, bring out the best, share their joys and sorrows and create that genuine personal connection, which is very important to encourage teams to deliver with professionalism. I have always believed myself to be a team-member-leader concept. I owe my personal growth to the delivery excellence of the teams I was fortunate to lead. It was important for people to see that I could be hands-on working shoulder-to-shoulder with my teammates as well as assume leadership roles.

While working on these projects I also learned how to engage with the different stakeholders of a project, the most important being the client. Transparency, keeping commitments and never over-promising were some of the characteristics I learned from being on the job as well as from my mentors. This transparency also helped in building trust with the global clients I handled in different countries. This is what makes for authentic leadership.

Having the right talent for the right job, creating a culture of transparency and fairness all became the building blocks of creating trust in leadership. This will always hold true. It has helped me to lead two major transformations of global technology organizations.

In fact, I had been part of three transformations. The first was when PwC, the world's number one audit firm, was becoming a consulting and advisory services organization in information technology. The second was when IBM, a global technology icon, was transforming itself into an IT services company. The third organization was Ericsson, the world's leading telecom equipment company, becoming an Information Communication and Technology (ICT) organization, competing with Indian and global IT services companies and meeting the IT requirements of its telecom clients.

In the first organization, I was a member of the orchestra when I watched keenly how the conductors were going about their job. From being a team member, I created my own teams and took part in building the strategic direction of the firm. My second assignment led me to understand how to help steer a massive ocean liner in a 180-degree turn and make it as nimble as a jet ski, while at the same time retaining the advantage of its size.

The most exciting and challenging part of my assignment was to transform organizations that were all over 100 years old. It was a unique experience of how centurions reinvented their competitive advantage. It was all about understanding the importance of rich heritage, respecting the culture of the people who built the foundation, earning their trust through transparency and fairness and making them a part of the new journey. Believe me, no management school can teach these skills. It has to come from your upbringing of being empathetic to others, respect for the contribution of your predecessors and encouraging new talent to become leaders. It was about creating entirely new organizations out of an edifice of century-old institutions.

I had undergone a personal transformation, from being a player in the orchestra to conducting it. The job of a leader is not all about creating a success story; it is also about accepting blame when things don't go as per plan. To me, this has been an amazing journey. I have learned, unlearned and re-learned at every step of the way. It has had its due share of highs and lows. I have been unsuccessful in managing some of the relationships and I wished I had done better. I have had incredible teams with fire in the belly to support me.

I consider myself fortunate to have the humbling experience of being a part of those teams and to have led them. My commitment to them has always been that I am there to take care of things when they aren't going right. When teams have this air cover of responsible leadership, trust me, they can achieve the impossible. This is the kind of non-intrusive leadership that I constantly strive to achieve.

Leadership is also about setting examples. It is not always about doing big things that make headlines. It is also about small touches that make a big change. The iconic chief of Tata Steel, Mr Russi Mody, has been the subject of several anecdotes about how his personal touch of leadership created a big difference. Legend has it that Mody once discovered that the officers' toilet in the organization was very clean, while the staff toilet was rather unhygienic. In those days, having separate toilets wasn't considered discriminatory. He asked how long it would take to have both toilets equally clean and hygienic. Mody's officers told him that it would take a month or so. He replied that it could be done in an hour if someone would call a carpenter. Though visibly taken aback, the facilities head immediately got a man with the carpentry tools. Mody asked the workman to just interchange the signboards from staff to officers' – the job was done!

Chapter 9

I Have no Plans and no Plans to Plan

Our professional and personal survival has never been tested as it is now in this COVID-normal world. Each day is a new trial and test of fortitude. The big question that hovers in everyone's mind: When will things be normal? No one knows the answer. We're flying blind, but not exactly if we know how to navigate uncertainty. It isn't an existential crisis, but an opportunity to rediscover our relevancies in an ambiguous world, in a world where goalposts are changing by the day.

For the last several years, we have been waiting for 2020 as if there was something magical about it. It was a milestone with a sci-fi ring to the numbers. Forecasts like computers with consciousness, robots taking over the world and most of our jobs, nanobots surfing through our bloodstreams deciding and controlling the calories we need haven't really happened.

However, remarkable strides have been made in the human-computer interface. Advances in food technology ushering in meatless burgers, promises of sending tourists into outer space more real than ever before, artificial intelligence permeating several aspects of our lives and drones delivering medicines to remote areas have all taken place in the last few years, creating an exciting platform for 2020 to introduce even more incredible things. And then it happened. The pandemic created a dystopian world and untold human tragedy struck. All our plans went topsy-turvy. It created a paradox – lives or livelihood.

COVID-19 put digital transformation on steroids, compressing timelines of technology maturity from decades to months. This is making the task of forecasting even more challenging. Without sticking my neck out, all I can say is that this decade, starting with 2020, is going to be the most exciting phase of our lives, which will set the pace for the next five years or so. Can we plan for it? Or is it better to work out an agile and adaptive strategy based on continuous analysis of the unfolding transformative or disruptive powers?

All our lives, we have been told that failing to plan is like planning to fail. Here I am, with over three decades in the information technology industry, persisting along, working out how to meet the challenges or ride the opportunities of the day as it comes by. I take each day as it comes. There is no template to navigate the next as analogies of the past won't work in the future. The reality that we've got is much messier than what we're promised.

Years ago, as a college kid on a trip to some unknown forest with friends, a group of us lost our way in the woods. We were without a map and no idea where we were. As kids seldom think about consequences and therefore treading where angels fear, we went along, following our instincts guided by a general sense of where the path back to our campsite should be. There was no track to follow, perhaps no one had been there before us. As we plodded along, we heard the faint sound of gurgling water. As thirsty as we were, that seemed an innate direction to follow. Suddenly, the jungle cleared and before us lay a stunningly beautiful grassland with a stream flowing happily over rocks and pebbles.

We forgot our troubles, took off our clothes and splashed around in the water. Eventually, we did get back as some shepherds who were grazing their cattle in the grasslands guided us to our campsite. We had a great time entertaining our friends, who were waiting anxiously for us, with stories of our adventure. I added a little bit of imagination to it to make them even more jealous.

A fork in my career path

Much later in a Big Four consulting firm, I came to a fork in the path of my career – to tread into an unknown trail and take on challenges as they came or to stick to the tried-and-tested known environment, working with people I had always been working with and continuing to do what I was doing – a very comfortable existence. This time, I deliberately chose the unknown track in the forest, broke away from my comfort zone and launched myself with a handful of teammates to create something that didn't exist.

There was a financial rehabilitation project for a cement manufacturing company in Kathmandu in Nepal, funded by KfW Development Bank, a German financial institution, which was awarded to Price Waterhouse, the consulting firm I was employed in. It had run into huge challenges as the team had architected a rather complicated IT solution that was both time consuming and difficult to implement.

It had caused a severe delay in the implementation, resulting in funds almost running out without showing any tangible outcome. The choice for my company was to exit the project, thereby risking blacklisting, or quickly fix the architectural issues and deliver the project with a shortened timeframe and within the leftover budget. When I was offered this project to manage, I also had another proposal to run an assignment that was using Fourth Generation Language using RDBMS, which was the latest at that point in time. On the other hand, the project in Nepal was based on legacy FoxPro.

I walked over to my boss, Mr Roopendra Narayan Roy, the CEO of PwC's consulting business, and asked him bluntly which project was more important for the organization. Without hesitation, he said it was the Nepal project. Right there, I decided to launch myself and my small team into this engagement with a single-minded dedication to give it my best to revive it.

To this day, it gives me huge satisfaction on having taken up that assignment, and I remain ever so thankful to Mr Roy for letting me take up a project that was almost given up. It proved to be a turning point in my life. I suffered health challenges, family issues and various other non-work-related problems, but we battled through it all to turn it around. This was an opportunity I created, and it helped build my reputation in the organization. That was the beginning, in many ways, of my future career path.

I have always believed in simplifying problems by breaking them up into smaller, more manageable chunks and solving each of those one at a time. This makes the big problem look less daunting. The manager who was running that project handed me a very complicated and detailed Microsoft Project Plan, which was perhaps a perfect plan in every respect. The only challenge was that the project was going haywire because too much effort had gone into planning without a similar focus on execution. Ever since taking over the project, he used to check whether I updated his Project Plan, which he had taken much pride in creating and maintaining.

Get the project done

When Mr Roy wanted a status report on the project, as there was a complaint that I wasn't updating the project plan with all the hourly updates of tasks and sub-tasks, I bluntly told him that he had to give me a choice – either keep updating the Microsoft Project plan or execute the project. The answer came promptly – get the project done. I threw out the plan and dove into execution and gave it all I had to make it flawless. This project, for my organization at that point, was critical as this was one of the first large IT transformation engagements outside India. The success of it would have marked our entry into IT services and significantly lifted the morale of the organization. It wouldn't have happened if my boss hadn't lent me his unstinted support.

I had a firm belief that opportunities appear before all of us and how we identify them makes all the difference between success and failure. Though I didn't have much faith in too much planning or strategizing about my career, I felt that there was an exciting opportunity to create something new here. I didn't know what the outcome would eventually turn out to be. The sheer excitement of doing something that hasn't been done before – being a part of a team transforming a century-old iconic global organization – was far too seductive to ignore. It was enough to leave my safe shores and sail for the unknown. Ships, as they say, are not built to be docked in a safe harbor! I chose to live in that moment.

There is no way of knowing how life will turn out and uncertainties lurk at every corner. Each day presents us with situations we haven't encountered before, and we have to find solutions to those. Life is always giving us tests first and then teaching us the lessons, quite the opposite of what we did in our school days.

Does this mean that I'm against thinking about the future and being prepared for it? Of course not. Horizon thinking is a positive approach to understand which way business trends, technology currents and macroeconomic issues are shaping up. These are inputs that one gathers to get a general sense of the direction to move, like the time we were lost in the forest and the sound of a stream guided us toward it. However, it should not lead to too much planning and basing your preparedness on that plan because things might not work out the way you have foreseen as the velocity of change is outpacing all our well-laid-out plans. However, one must have a north star to guide, a big-picture strategy showing the direction. As Roman philosopher, Seneca, said, "If one does not know to which port one is sailing, no wind is favorable."

Agile planning

If you look at the Fortune 100 list, you'll find that in the ten years between 2008 and 2018, it has changed dramatically with 43 of the companies dropping out of the list. At the same time, Walmart, which ranked as the largest company in the world in 2008 with $379 billion in revenue, remained at #1 in 2018 with over $500 billion in revenue. It continued to top the charts in 2019. When the entry of Amazon's online shopping disrupted Walmart, it quickly got its act together to invest in creating a rival digital experience for its customers. It shifted strategies, significantly reducing spending on building new stores in favor of growing online, lowering prices and adding more services in physical stores such as online grocery pickup. It was a perfectly executed pivot for a traditional brick-n-mortar chain store, an instance of agile planning.

This kind of rapid planning and fast execution will be business as usual in this COVID-normal world. No organization can survive without these skills. Take, for example, the entertainment industry. Netflix is producing and screening its own movies, which is now challenging the established theater industry. Esports, a digital interactive multiplayer video game competition, with participants from across the world, are threatening traditional sports like cricket or even football. The pandemic has rushed in these technologies that we felt would take some more years to mature. The advent of augmented and virtual reality technologies is taking interactivity to newer heights of experience in these games. Every sport played in the physical stadiums now must be redesigned for the digital space. These are just a few examples of how our known world is changing without giving us a warning. This is where nimble planning will become mission-critical to turn a potential disaster into a triumph. Sporting events have always given us instances of dramatically fluctuating fortunes, stunning defeats and even remarkable turnarounds, all examples of the ability to rapidly change plans or the failure to do so.

Nimble leadership

Rahul Dravid was being given saline in the dressing room. The sweltering March heat at the Eden Gardens in Kolkata, a beautiful cricket stadium, was taking a heavy toll on the batsman who had scored a century and was on a record-breaking stand with his colleague at the other end, VVS Laxman, who went on to score 281 – the highest ever till then by an Indian batsman. In the first innings, India was dismissed for a meager 190 runs with Australia scoring 400. The 2000-01 India-Australia test series was poised for a most dramatic climax. It was to enter the list of legendary matches ever played.

On 15th January 2009, US Airways Flight 1549 lost power to both engines shortly after take-off from LaGuardia Airport upon striking a large flock of geese. Captain Chesley Sullenberger realized they would not make it back to an airport. There was no time to plan. Captain Sully had seen the birds three seconds before they were sucked into the engine of his Airbus A320 carrying 155 passengers.

The cricket test match was all but over for the young skipper, Sourav Ganguly, who had just lost the earlier match at Mumbai. He had only recently taken over the team after a cloud of match-fixing had cast a dark shadow over the players, and the future of Indian cricket was in serious doubt. India was facing one of the finest Aussie teams studded with some of the greatest players of all time.

The Airbus A320 that Sully and his co-pilot, Jeff Skiles, were flying was a 'fly-by-wire' aircraft, which meant the pilots did not directly control the plane's movement. Being machine-controlled, it required a power supply for the pilots to take control. In that circumstance, the pilots of Flight 1549 had no way of controlling the aircraft. They could not go up and down nor left or right. The plane was literally falling out of the sky and the captain and his co-pilot had barely a few minutes to decide how to save the passengers.

Ganguly didn't have much of a plan, except keeping at it doggedly session by session. It took a monumental effort between Rahul and Laxman as the pair batted all day, taking India from 254 for 4 wickets to 589 for 4 and setting up one of the greatest test match comebacks of all time – a 171 run victory for India after following on. The newly inducted spinner, Harbhajan Singh, had a dream run, taking three wickets with consecutive balls to shape up India's unbelievable victory over a team that was unbeaten in their 16 previous test matches.

Captain Sully attempted something he had never done or even practiced before. At 15:29:28, two minutes and 18 seconds after the bird strike, his voice came over at the control tower at La Guardia, which was trying to direct him. "We're gonna be in the Hudson," he said in the calmest possible manner. At the deposition later, before an official investigation committee, examining his actions that day he said, "This was a novel event that we had never trained for. Yet I was able to set clear priorities. I took what I did know, adapted it and applied it in a new way to solve a problem I'd never seen before." He knew that the Hudson River was the only widest and smoothest stretch that could land the A320. Luck was on his side that day.

Luck played a huge factor for Harbhajan too, who got a chance to play in that match as Anil Kumble, the prime spin weapon in India's arsenal, was injured earlier and had to be dropped. "The world wouldn't have known me if Anil was not injured," Harbhajan had quipped once. Luck shines on every one of us at some point in our career or other. The difference between success and failure is how we take the opportunity and turn it into a success.

Create your own luck

During my childhood, I was a great fan of Bruce Lee, the legendary martial arts superstar, who didn't believe in pure luck. He once said, "You have to create your own luck. You have to be aware of the opportunities around you and take advantage of them." Luck happens to each one of us. As

Eliyahu Goldratt rightly points out, "Good luck is when opportunity meets preparation, while bad luck is when lack of preparation meets reality."

I consider myself lucky in many ways. My upbringing in a middle-class household of working parents is also part of my luck. It taught me the realities of life. It taught me that everything I achieve is a bonus. It taught me never to take anything for granted. That I wasn't ever going to get into a premier management institute was also a huge luck factor. I learned how to overcome that shortcoming and develop my other areas of strength. I was lucky to be the right man at the right time when challenges happened in the organizations I worked for. But one has to make luck happen.

My luckiest day was when I met my mentor, Dr. Samir Sadhukhan of IIM-Calcutta. He taught me computer programming at his humble home in a narrow lane at Baghbazar in North Calcutta. He held my hand like I was his younger brother and gave me everything he knew. From him, I learned a rare leadership skill – the amazing desire to help others.

Humility of knowledge

The other lesson was the importance of genuine humility despite being one of the best in your field. As they say, the weight of real knowledge makes your head bow in reverence to the vast unknown oceans of knowledge before you. With every new piece of knowledge that you acquire, you realize how much you don't know, and hence, the humility.

I was stuck in a project in Ganjam district in the Indian state of Odisha. There was a bug in the program that I couldn't figure out. I turned to Dr Sadhukhan for help. In those days, I could only afford to send him an unreserved general compartment railway ticket to come to my aid. Dr Sadhukhan happily came to his student's assistance and solved the problem. That's a leadership lesson I will never forget in my life. It has stayed with me forever. Every now and then, when someone meets me or drops by my office, seeking some kind of assistance, I remember my mentor. He never turned away anyone who sought his help. Helping without expecting anything in return, not even gratitude, is how we build our bank of good wishes. Someday, it'll work out for us, like it has for me.

Leadership is about giving your best every day and taking life one day at a time. It is impossible to plan for every situation. It is difficult to predict what your day is going to be like. The unexpected will happen when it is least expected. You can't use experience for something you haven't experienced.

Sometimes, situations bring out the leadership qualities in us that we ourselves do not know existed. My leadership lessons have been experiential, leading me to believe with almost religious conviction the time-tested philosophy of 'one day at a time', working for the outcome and not for the income that one receives as a remuneration at the end of the month or for the bonuses. Staying focused on delivering the best performance on the job given is the surest way to succeed and be happy. Personally, I have never planned my career goal.

Taking each day as it comes

My objective was to do so well in the work given to me that the next challenging assignment would automatically come to me and would become another stepping-stone to move on. I avoid the word 'move ahead' because that's not what I work for. My work is about taking immense pleasure in doing a job to the best of my ability and doing better than my best and not bother about whether I have been rewarded for it or not. It's a no-plan plan that has worked wonderfully for me all these years.

The Australians, having the best cricket team at that point in time and considered almost invincible, lost to the Indians because they wanted to win so desperately that they became overconfident about their ability to wipe the opponents out cheaply twice. It didn't occur to them that the Indians might force them to bat a fourth inning on a wicket that was crumbling at Eden's, which was exactly what happened. By contrast, the Indian skipper worked every over, each session, one at a time, using his resources optimally without thinking of the end goal. Sourav later confessed that he had kept his mind sharply focused on the immediate in that remarkable test, hailed as one of the biggest turnarounds in cricket history.

Taking each day as it comes and doing the best is the only way in today's rapidly changing technology and business landscape. Change is actually not the correct word; it is a radical transformation that we see around us in a COVID-normal world. It is happening at an incredible velocity, completely unsettling the old ways of doing things. We have entered the great era of discomfort in an exponential world. At the same time, no one can say that this was how it has always been done before. It is a great opportunity to create afresh.

If you want to stay relevant in this period of great disruption, then it should be remembered that one should learn to accept it as growth and comfort never coexisted. The levels of complexities we face in our organizations, personal lives and societies are unprecedented. The only way to stay relevant is through a constant process of learning, unlearning and relearning. As Arie de Gues famously wrote in 1988, the ability to learn faster than your competition is your only sustainable competitive advantage, as what we learn today is no longer relevant tomorrow.

We must constantly figure out our 'art of staying relevant'. For one to stay relevant, one will constantly need to invest in oneself through learning. Five hours of learning every day are what leaders have followed for themselves. I have personally benefited from it immensely. From morning till late evening, we work for our companies to help them accomplish their targets. Similarly, every day, we need to put aside a few hours for our own development to accomplish personal targets. I have made it a habit to spend a couple of hours post-dinner reading whatever I want. It's a great tool to enhance one's knowledge base. I would strongly recommend it.

"Nearly 50% of subject knowledge acquired during the first year of a four-year technical degree becomes outdated by the time students graduate." – an alarming statement coming from the World Economic Forum in a report on the future of work. We can debate on the percentages or split hair on the details, but let me tell you that those of us who think that this change is very fast, wait till you have seen what is coming.

Way back in the winter of 2015, I was at an event addressing a group of young information technology professionals. I began my presentation with a piece of Western classical music and asked the audience if they knew who the artist was. When I told them that a robot had composed the music and was also playing it, there was stunned disbelief among the listeners.

I was trying to explain how computers could be trained to perform even creative work and that very soon, our existing skills would become redundant unless we updated ourselves. There were a few in the audience who rubbished the idea and perhaps felt their present skills made them recession-proof. By the next winter, some of them had joined the ranks of those whose jobs were being automated and they were trying to reinvent themselves mid-career.

Reinventing relevancy in a crisis

No matter what you do today, you can count on the fact that it will not be around in ten years. The future is no longer a linear progression of what you have done in the past. It has become exponential and this calls for exponential thinking. In 1965, Gordon Moore, the co-founder of Intel, made an observation that became Moore's Law, which states that the number of transistors on a microchip doubles in about every two years though the cost of computers gets halved. This exponential growth in computing speed has been driving most technological changes around us in an exponential way.

Let me explain further. If you take 30 steps linearly, you will walk 30 meters. But if you take 30 doubling steps, going one meter in the first step, then two meters, then four, then eight and so on, by step 30, you will have traveled one billion meters or 26 times around the globe – that is the exponential kind of growth. The future ahead of us will not be linear; it is exponential.

It is not just technical knowledge that is getting disrupted at laser speed. Everything around us is in a constant state of a high degree of fluidity that we haven't witnessed before. Corporate pecking orders are being changed overnight. The oil giants, like Exxon, or industrial behemoths, like GE, have been replaced by technology companies like Apple, Microsoft, Amazon, Google, Facebook or Netflix in the key stock indexes. In India, we see OnePlus, a fairly new entrant in the booming smartphone market, upstaging market leaders, Samsung and Apple, in a matter of just a few years to dominate the business.

During the span of my career, I have witnessed how organizations and the skills of individuals were disrupted and how they reinvented themselves to come back again faster, leaner and increasingly more competitive. This has forced us to acquire the most important skill, the art of staying relevant. Ice hockey great Wayne Gretzky's father once told him, "Go to where the puck is going, not where it has been."

Dozens of research reports in the last few years have come up with different skill requirements to achieve continuous relevancy. What they all say is that Complex Problem Solving is among the top requirements in the list. This brings us to the critical question of defining the problem. Identifying the problem that we are trying to solve becomes the most critical skill that will see us at our competitive best.

"It's not that I'm so smart; it's just that I stay with problems longer." This is what the smartest man spanning generations, Albert Einstein, had once remarked. It reflects his amazing humility, but the real message is embedded in the last part of the statement. "…I stay with the problem longer." Unravel the problem, peel away its layers and explore it from all possible angles and you are already half-way through thinking the solution.

"I am not afraid to ask dumb questions," the former US President, Barrack Obama, had once remarked, explaining how, as a leader of the world's most powerful nation, he makes decisions. It is this humility to accept that you cannot have all the answers yourself that creates smart leadership. Surround yourself with the best minds, especially those who dare to disagree with you.

I am, by nature, a collector of good people around me in my inner circle. They have helped me to stay grounded, have been strong enough to challenge me when they felt I was wrong and debated with me with conviction, logic, reasoning and data and not only opinions. However, these are very rare people. At the same time, one must accept that one cannot change people, but you can change the people around you.

Generation Z – those born around the mid to late nineties – will comprise the bulk of customers and employees by 2030. This is a socially conscious generation that will demand transparent and authentic leadership. Some of these young people are even becoming CEOs in their early twenties. The challenge for leadership will be to look at problems through the lens of its impact on humanity. Etched in my memory is a visual of Princess Diana shaking the hands of an AIDS patient way back in 1987 without wearing gloves. In one striking moment, it changed people's perception of the disease forever.

It is the difference between a human being and being human that will define leadership as Gen Z will demand it, and they will be our key stakeholders. With 50% of our existing jobs disappearing from technological disruptions, leaders must humanize the problems. No solution, whether political or corporate, can be designed that does not address human impact. This is the essence of design thinking in leadership. Humanizing a problem will be putting human needs first in anything you design or any decision you take.

From using sensors to assess the fertilizer requirements in soil, helping farmers optimize resources and creating sustainable agriculture to something as simple as changing the email ID under contacts from *contacts@companyname.com* to *amitabh@companyname.com* defines the concept of humanizing solutions. Our products, services and decisions must create an experience for users that makes them feel like there's a person, not a machine, at the other end of the connection. While we cannot plan with certainty in a highly dynamic scenario as we face today, we can keep these basic principles as our guiding lights in visualizing the way before us.

No matter the terminology used, the leadership of the future must grapple with unprecedented changes for which there exists no template. And in this context, the emergent leadership style of learning by doing better than the best you can, every day, each moment, is perhaps going to be the mantra to stay relevant and deliver value to the organization to people and our planet.

The world is fluid in a way, and so is the leader's role. It has shifted from predicting, planning and allocating tasks to observing, fashioning a highly accommodative and elastic work environment, inspiring and empowering the workforce and providing them with both the necessary will and skill to perform. Above all, leadership is about flawless execution. I have tried to explain this to many of my junior colleagues that a grand vision without execution is a fatal flaw in the thinking. This is a mistake I saw several times in my career. Three things are essential for success – execution, execution and execution.

Once again, I am lucky to not have started my career with a management degree from a reputed institute or an engineering qualification from the premier colleges where most of my peers have graduated from. They are the finest brains I have worked with, but at times, I noticed that their education had fueled a huge ambition and pushed them toward setting achievement goals and planning a career roadmap. I thought that it put an enormous amount of pressure on themselves to achieve their goals, overtake their peers in the race to the top. On the contrary, I focused on doing the best every day in any job I was assigned to. I still follow the same principle.

The no-plan doing your best each day at a time has worked for me. I have no plans and no plans to plan either. The only plan that has worked for me is to place the organization's goals ahead of any personal career goals and make them mine. Right now, our goals are to survive the crisis and create the foundations to thrive again.

The organization, Ericsson, I currently work for is providing the critical lifeline of communications when we are physically distancing. We're helping people, families, organizations to stay connected. I am focused on delivering it flawlessly, every day, day after day. If we can do that honestly and efficiently, meeting the needs of our customers and people, the outcome will help us to thrive even in this volatile world. My entire focus is on doing what is right always whether there is a crisis or not, rather than following the process book, which tells me how to do things right. Right now, it is keeping the world connected, preparing the organization for tomorrow and ensuring we have the skills to deliver excellence.

Chapter 10

Theory of Relativity – The Emergency

The phone kept ringing in my pocket, and every now and then, I had to disconnect it. I was in the midst of a serious presentation to the leaders of PwC in the boardroom, reviewing the firm's financials and profit commitments before the year-end. This was the third missed call from my home number in less than ten minutes. It made me a little jittery. Someone from home was trying to urgently reach me, unmindful of the fact that I was repeatedly disconnecting the calls. My standard instruction for my family was that they don't call me at the office unless it was an emergency. For anything important, one missed call from their end would suffice; I would call back at my first available window.

As the audience took a short breather during one of the slides to debate the contents among themselves, I excused myself and stepped outside the room to take the call. I could sense that my seniors weren't too happy with this interruption in the flow of such an important presentation. At the other end was my six-and-half-year-old son's desperate voice. He almost screamed that he wanted to talk to me on an urgent and important matter. I asked him if it could wait until I finished my work or if he had something really pressing.

"It is urgent," my son said, almost hysterically.

Now, I was worried. "Is everything okay at home?" I asked.

He brushed my question aside and launched straight into his problem. "The internet isn't working; there's no connection," he blurted out, almost in a state of heightened agitation.

I calmly reminded him of our rule of not calling me at work unless it was an emergency that needed my immediate presence or intervention of sorts.

"It *is* an emergency, Baba; the internet is not working," he almost wailed. How I could not classify this as an emergency was beyond my son.

Stepping back to get perspective

It took me a while to step into my son's shoes and look at things from his perspective. To him and his generation, being always connected was like oxygen. I remembered that during our last family holiday, the first thing the kids had asked the hotel receptionist was for the Wi-Fi password. This was Gen Z, the 'always on' generation. Well, I must admit that my son's interruption did break the rhythm of my presentation, but nevertheless, I assured him that I would call the support helpline and get them to fix the internet. These days, during work from home, such interruptions from kids are considered normal. Newscasters in global television channels have been reading the news while cradling kids in their arms.

After disconnecting the call, I called the helplines, booked a complaint and returned to the boardroom to continue with the presentation after apologizing to the audience for the interruption. I explained that I had to take the call as there was an 'emergency' at home. Inwardly, I held back a chuckle realizing how my scope of an emergency has just expanded!

We often face similar challenges in our day-to-day lives and our responses need to be measured. Otherwise, we can create conflicts or misunderstandings. A momentary pause to understand the other person's point of view is critical if we must resolve a problem. This was about being sensitive to others; it was about being compassionate. It all depends on our ability to comprehend another person's psychological experiences – thoughts, feelings and attitudes.

Conflict resolution

But why think this way? With a plateful of complications for every individual, why must we add to the confusion by considering opposing views? The answer is simple: It helps us resolve conflicts constructively. What we forget every time in a conflicting situation is that everyone involved in the conflict has a unique point of view. No two people will see a situation or issue in exactly the same way. Successful problem-solvers are people who can hold all opposing ideas, positions and perspectives in their minds at the same time and still function effectively. More importantly, they have this ability to identify a common string amidst all that contradictory jumble.

We must accept that relativity is much underrated yet crucial. The degree of importance, nature of urgency, even at times what is right or wrong, is relative. One major conflict in almost every home while watching TV is also because of this. If we are interested in a certain kind of show or movie, we assume that everyone – at least in our circle of acquaintance – would share similar preferences. Or if we like a particular sport, we assume everyone likes it too! Sounds juvenile as I write this, but come to think of it, most of us would love the world to revolve according to our fancy.

It is also true that the same person might have a different point of view at different times. As our experiences, knowledge, assumptions, job role and values change, our preferences, perspectives and choices change too. Over the years, between when I started my career and now, what I seek from my job has changed. It started with getting opportunities to work on the right technology and good projects. Thereafter, it moved to financial security as being a priority to today, working exclusively on what makes me happy!

My mother's faith in religion

Points of view can create bias. It is human nature that once we develop an opinion or a perspective, we tend to seek out only the information that confirms it, often ignoring facts that might be contradictory to our point of view. We generally avoid those who challenge our perspective. This is confirmation bias. Researchers have recently conducted studies to determine if the issue of confirmation bias is as prevalent as it seems.

In one experiment, participants chose to either support or oppose a given socio-political issue. They were then presented with evidence that was conflicting, affirming or a combination of both. In all the scenarios, participants proved most likely to stick with their initial decisions. When presented with conflicting evidence, just one in five changed their stance. Moreover, participants who maintained their initial view became even more confident in the superiority of their decision – proof of how potent confirmation bias can be.

Today, social media users are faced with an overwhelming number of news sources, which vary widely in reliability and honesty. Fake news takes advantage of social media by using sensationalist headlines and making unproven claims. Readers viewing these incorrect articles find some of them aligned with their own biased outlooks and re-post or share them, further spreading the half-truths or fully distorted misinformation.

My mother was very devoted to her religion and god. Due to her unwavering devotion, god used to take all the credit for everything good that happened in our family, be it me passing an examination or recovering after a mild flu. Whenever any good news arrived, she would touch her forehead with folded hands and announce with due reverence, "By god's grace." However, I never saw god take any responsibility if anything bad ever happened in our household. This was my first encounter with bias.

In my opinion, the further you can mentally distance yourself from a problem, the better will you be able to see the problem. A broader view of the picture helps one to get a grip on diverse elements in the landscape. Let's take this example about how distancing can give you a completely different view.

As organizations, we often fight in the office between verticals and horizontals, business unit vs geography, different P&L owners with conflicting priorities and so on. These are all about boundaries. When you go further, detach yourself from the organizational cocoon, you get a very different outlook. An outsider – like customers – being far away from our organization, doesn't see those borders because they get blurred with distance. Hence, they see us as one company. But from inside, we can see many small units inside a large organization fighting over boundary issues.

Authority bias

In my career, I have often come across something called the authority bias. We are more likely to trust and be influenced by ideas that come from authority figures. We rarely think of challenging these ideas or even questioning them or putting them to test. This creates echo chambers around people of authority, which can be extremely poisonous for organizations. It prevents the free flow of thoughts and ideas, stifling creativity and innovation.

I would like to point out that having a bias is a natural human trait. Either consciously or unconsciously, our minds are prone to classify situations, things and people into comfortable and uncomfortable zones. Such classifications often have no apparent logic and may originate from deep-rooted subconscious cues. Whatever their origin may be, bias invariably leads to decisions that are one-sided, unreasonable and partial. This is especially true in the workplace.

Bias at work usually takes the form of irrational judgment – either on individuals or corporate decisions. Between employees, bias can create discrimination on the grounds of gender, age, orientation, religion, caste, ethnicity, physical attributes, special needs and infirmities. Antagonism or insults based on any of the above spells doom for work culture. It is counterproductive and stops a company from being diverse and inclusive in terms of the talent pool.

In my various roles at different organizations, I have tried to encourage my teammates to create an environment where we can challenge each other in friendly fights so that we can come up with a bullet-proof idea. I never thought of myself as the fountainhead of all wisdom because I clearly understand my limitations. My entire objective is to steer the discussion toward a consensus of the best ideas, coming from minds that are capable of accepting viewpoints that might differ from their own.

Above all, I encourage myself and others who work with me to question their own biases; that is the starting point. Once we recognize our biases, we can ourselves work out the answers. In the process, we will automatically figure out a way to resolve conflicts, create innovative solutions and nurture relationships both at home and at work.

Later that evening, driving back from the office, I started thinking about the whole situation in the afternoon and realized how each event is relative in terms of where we stand and watch them. Of course, for a six-and-a-half-year-old, the internet is the window to a world of knowledge, entertainment and amusement, all reaching him over a pair of twisted copper wire. That incident had taught me a lot. Reality can be so complex that equally valid observations from different points of view can appear to be contradictory. It all depends on where you stand. If you draw a six on a piece of paper, it will look like a nine to the person standing opposite to you. When I reached home, I was received with a warm hug. The internet problem was fixed, and everybody was happy.

Finding a method in this madness

Our life is buffeted with conflicts, contradictions and relativity. I ask myself what kind of behavior would make one survive during troubles. It's madness all around, and we need to find a method around the madness. Here are a few things I try to follow so as to preserve my sanity during times when I need to rationalize things and when I am challenged with the theory of relativity or managing conflicting perspectives:

- **Take a break.** A break is a helpful tool. You can take a break and remain engaged at the same time. It is a method that can be used to create some room to think through the situation when you have a deadlock or stalemate. I have noticed that most successful people have trouble pulling back from their obsessive focus on the problem at hand. In fact, for many, being focused was their key to their success. So they rely on their tried-and-tested method but fail to understand that focus is not enough at times. Pausing in action can lead to greater creativity and efficiency.
- **You don't know what you don't know.** We need to tell ourselves that someone else may have a better idea about something we are struggling with. There might always be an opportunity to learn something new or find a different perspective from someone I never expected. A new idea that can solve my problem or a method being used in a different industry might be the solution for me in the current situation. Listening and thinking from a place of not knowing is a critical means of encouraging the discovery of original, unexpected and breakthrough ideas.
- **Ask the right question.** Even after having tried your level best and spending more than enough time, if you remain trapped in a problem without any solution, a way forward can be to reconsider the questions you are asking yourself. Relook at the problem itself that you are trying to solve. Asking yourself a different set of questions might help unblock your existing mental model.

If a software project delivery is getting delayed, the solution might not lie hidden in a lack of productivity or planning. Just throwing in some additional resources may not solve the issue if the real problem is team motivation. You will have to ask the right questions to understand the real issue and solve it.

- **Clarity about your direction.** In today's complex environment, it is important to set our direction and not necessarily destination. When working with a team, I think direction becomes more important than the destination. Destination, the pretty big picture, can be overwhelming and distract one from concentrating on the small steps that are needed to reach there. Leadership is a journey along with your team, guided by purpose and vision – mere objectives are not enough. Remember, the journey is also important, and one should enjoy it on its way to the goal. Focusing too much on the goal will create unnecessary stress and you may miss your path.

  Almost always, I bring the team together to get something difficult done; I tell them the problem and ask them to have their own solutions to achieve the goal. One will have to trust their team and believe that they are not the smartest person in the room. And if you are indeed the smartest person in the room, I suggest that you change the room immediately.

- **Five whys.** The 'Five Whys' technique was first developed by Taiichi Ohno, the creator of Lean Manufacturing, as a way of determining the root cause of a problem. It is a simple and effective tool for solving problems. Born in Dalian, China, Taiichi was the main architect of the Toyota Production System. He described the Five Whys method as "the basis of Toyota's scientific approach by repeating 'why' five times the nature of the problem, as well as its solution, becomes clear."

  Quite simply, you ask 'why?' five times, each time going deeper into the previous answer. Five times is just a prevalent convention, formulated on a typical anecdotal number of repetitions usually required to arrive at the root cause. You are free to continue beyond five to suit your requirements. Let's take two examples:

Situation 1 – A client is unhappy

- 1st Why – Because we could not deliver the software delivery project on time.
- 2nd Why – The interfaces were too many, so development took longer.
- 3rd Why – We underestimated the number of interfaces and the complexity involved.
- 4th Why – We did not list all the details during the pre-proposal fact-finding.
- 5th Why – We had quarter closing pressure and could not devote enough attention to the details and had to close the deal in a hurry (this is the root cause).

Situation 2 – The vehicle will not start

- 1st Why – The battery is dead.
- 2nd Why – The alternator is not functioning.
- 3rd Why – The alternator belt was broken.
- 4th Why – The alternator belt was well beyond its useful service life and not replaced.
- 5th Why – The vehicle was not maintained, according to the recommended service schedule (the root cause).

As I said before, there might not be exactly five 'whys'. Five is an arbitrary number to remind you to dig deeper into the problem and get past the surface explanation. Running through five rounds of analysis, however, is usually enough to get to the crux of the matter.

Chapter 11

Doing the Right Things vs. Doing Things Right

Years ago, when I transitioned from being a team member to leading small teams, I came across my first paradox: the need to balance my instinct to seize the moment and the requirement to plan the day. Rigid planning went against my character, which was inclined toward being adaptive to factors I couldn't control and agile enough to pivot around to meet new challenges. The second paradox was to lead and be able to stay in the background at the same time. I found that unless teams were empowered, all decisions would have to come from me and that meant myself becoming a choke point. The third was to be a confident leader and concurrently be humble enough to accept that I wasn't the fountainhead of all wisdom.

Honestly, I didn't find it too difficult to find answers to these paradoxes. Once again, it came from my childhood experience. I had once skipped a very important class in college and went to watch a football match. A friend of mine covered for me during the roll call – what we called giving 'proxy'. Had he not done so, then I would have been in serious trouble as my attendance percentages were rather unflattering, to say the least. Later that evening, he gave me a dressing down for missing a critical class. But he also shared his notes with me.

He wasn't doing things right by giving me 'proxy', which saved me from being thrown out of class. It was clearly against the rules. However, he did the right thing by pointing out explicitly how wrong I was and at the same time, helping me with his notes after making me promise that I wouldn't repeat this. It was the answer to the paradoxes I faced – do the right thing. I followed my friend and have always slept peacefully with all my decisions.

Every once in a while, in our respective roles in our organizations, we come across a fork in the road when making decisions. We are faced with the choice of doing the right thing vs. doing things right. Often, we get confused about the difference between the two phrases. In my mind, it has always been rather simple – doing things right is mostly about following the processes while doing the right thing is about using our moral compasses to decide what is right, not only for the organization but also for the people who worked there. It benefited society and certainly was in the interest of the stakeholders.

This is something that will never change regardless of the sweeping transformations going on around us. In fact, this is going to become even more important in the future as technological transformations will create paradoxes that we have never encountered before. How do you become a leader who ushers in new technology and yet continue to be people friendly? How do you introduce automation and at the same time, be one of the best places to work for?

Organizations will continue to be run by people. Therefore, being sensitive to the aspirations and needs of people will always be important. The goods and services that organizations produce will be consumed by people. So understanding and being empathetic to the needs of people will continue to be the driving force of whatever we do. How can you be global and still local? How can you be a humble hero? These apparent paradoxes can only be answered by those who can choose the right fork in the path that lies before them.

Managers frequently choose to do things right as that is the tested path set down by the management of the organization, with little chances of going wrong. Even if things don't work out, we can always claim that we had adhered to the processes. But following your moral compass to do the right things can, at times, mean treading outside the sphere of processes and guidelines. This can be risky if the decisions do not work. In that case, there's no safety net of a process to shield the decision-maker from the unintended consequences even though the intention could have been right.

The moral compass

It's a twilight zone of decision-making, but I have often walked in that area guided by what I felt was the right thing to do, even though processes, guidelines and precedence were otherwise. This has constantly helped me build a far stronger organization with the people who lived the values and not just framed those bullet points for display in their offices.

Let me take an example, a fairly simple one at that. Deciding to invest in the normal illumination in the office that would save money or going for a more expensive one that would save the carbon footprint of the organization when the budget is tight and every rupee saved is precious. Common sense and short-term corporate objective would make us choose the less expensive but usual solution, which would easily be approved by the finance team. This is the path of least resistance. Who would debate and argue with the Chief Financial Officer over a few lighting options?

If I were deciding, I would select the energy-saving but initially more expensive option as in the long term, it will mean lower electricity bills and will help protect the environment. This will contribute toward being an environmentally conscious organization and create a brand as a green company. The payback of the initially more expensive option would come in the long term but would mean short-term sacrifice.

A slightly more complicated situation would be when one is faced with the option of selling the client a solution that we know is over-engineered for his requirement but meets the budgetary parameters and the sales team is almost certain to close the deal. The challenge for the leader is when they are aware that there is another solution that will be a perfect fit for the client, the infrastructure required would be less and maintenance wouldn't be expensive, but obviously, the selling organization would make less money on the contract.

A simple decision would be to let the sale of the more expensive solution go through if the customer is not objecting to it. An apparently silly choice would be to also place the less expensive but more appropriate solution/product before the customer and let him or her decide. This might create utter chaos in the selling organization. Most would see it as working against the interests of the company.

If the moral compass is followed and the right things are done, then one should take the option of placing both solutions before the customer. Even before that, a discussion should be held internally to give a solution that will be in the long-term interests of the customer. In all probability, the less expensive solution will win the day. Though the selling organization would make lower revenue on the sales, it will win the lifelong trust of the client and earn his loyalty, which would be far higher than the immediate revenue.

It would also avoid a situation where the customer would have found out later that a more suitable option existed that would have needed lesser investment. It could also prevent the customer from checking out alternatives with competitors. Even if they did, they would be convinced by the integrity of the organization they were dealing with. By presenting the alternative ourselves, we will not only earn the trust of the customer but become a lifelong partner for their organization. We would have also helped the customers' negotiating team to go back to their leadership to report a win-win deal for their organization.

Ethical judgment, which flows from having a moral compass, is learned and cultivated over the course of a career. It begins with an understanding of one's personal values. Crucible experiences are especially important to the development of a true North Star. I consider myself fortunate in this regard, having grown up in a middle-class humble family where these values were never taught explicitly but lived every day.

This is what you learn when you see your father return the extra money wrongly given to him by the vegetable seller lady who couldn't calculate well enough. It's about a friend admitting to the umpire that he hadn't caught the ball cleanly as it touched the ground before he took the catch, even though the most dangerous batsman had been given out. I guess these are simple things in life that stay with you even when you step into the world to make a living.

Be your own light

What I notice today, without being judgmental, is that many of us come from upwardly mobile backgrounds and that there is a sense of entitlement among them. They are driven fiercely by a combination of ambition because of their branded education and a high need for achievement because their social milieu judges them by their material triumphs and a lack of understanding about values. This can be a formula for disaster, even though they can have the best intentions.

There is a disconnect with the real India, its uniqueness, challenges, its accomplishments and failures that are not really understood or appreciated fully by those living cocooned lives in our high-rises. As a result, there is a lack of understanding about what really is a moral compass. I am sure that they will appreciate the value of the moral compass when they understand its true worth. Some people argue that values have to be viewed in the context of time and it can change over a period. In my opinion, values are carved in stone and will always remain constant regardless of all the changes happening around us.

We have to recognize that winning at all costs comes with a heavy price tag. We need to check the lodestar to see if we are headed in the right direction. Just check the real reasons behind the 2008 financial crisis and one will understand how extreme greed drove the world to a disaster from which we haven't yet fully recovered.

The fortunate part of this is that Generation Z, which is entering the workforce now, has a very high set of moral values. They are more interested to work for authentic leaders; they are worried about the fate of the planet. They have not known life without the internet, social networks or smartphones and are hyper-connected and will validate any information, cross-referencing several sources before accepting those on face value. In sharp contrast to the millennials, who are often described as the Me Generation, Gen Z rally around a variety of causes. They believe in dialogues to solve conflicts to improve the world and they have a strong moral compass to do the right things.

According to management guru Peter Drucker, "Management is doing things right; leadership is doing the right things." But the real tough decision to go by the moral compass is when it could mean risking everything you have ever achieved and not just money. Such things happen rarely but when they do, they become the stuff of corporate legends.

On a balmy June afternoon in 1978, LeMessurier (pronounced LeMeasure), one of the most celebrated American structural engineers, received a phone call from a young engineering student in New Jersey. It was no ordinary call. LeMessurier had, the year before, finished his iconic work – that of the construction of Citibank Corporation's new headquarters in Manhattan. The student was questioning Citicorp Tower's ability to withstand strong winds as the four columns that supported the skyscraper were in the wrong place. The 59-story skyscraper was an engineering marvel as it was built suspended above the church, standing on four stilts. This had to be done as the church wouldn't vacate the premises but agreed to sell the 'air' right above it.

The young student, while writing a paper on the famous building, had discovered a fatal design flaw in the construction, which could cause it to collapse in the middle of downtown New York. The engineer went back to the drawings and to his utter horror, discovered that there were indeed serious flaws in the design, which endangered the building. He started a review project aptly called 'Project SERENE'. The acronym stood for 'Special Engineering Review of Events Nobody Envisioned'. Several other design errors were discovered. He figured out a plan to wrap steel bands around the vulnerable areas of the building to prevent the crisis.

However, what he did next was even more remarkable. LeMessurier went ahead to call a press conference and openly declared the flaws and made all the necessary changes. Since he was the only one who knew about the problem, he could have stayed silent, but he chose to blow the whistle on himself, despite risks of massive financial damage from insurance claims and lawsuits. LeMessurier's behavior stands out as tall as his buildings for professional integrity and, above all, doing the right thing. His moral compass was working perfectly.

Every time we see such exemplary behavior, we stand up to salute the person. It is about doing things that showed you cared. It is about going beyond your defined duty, listening to the voice within you and acting in accordance.

What makes an entire country still remember, with fondness, a small, simple man from a farm who led the nation through its toughest times for barely 18 months? What makes every Indian proud when a self-effacing industrialist gives away nearly $21 billion from his wealth to charity over the years? The answer is simple; it's about having your heart in the right place; it's about having a moral compass – the lodestar of our character.

Lal Bahadur Shashtri took charge of the country as prime minister from Pandit Nehru, who was an English educated barrister from a very wealthy family. The enemy underestimated the new leader and attacked India. This diminutive politician from a very humble background unleashed the full force of the Indian army, scoring a remarkable victory in 1965.

However, he isn't remembered for just being a war-time prime minister, but a man who asked his family to forgo one meal every day so that they could feel the hunger pangs of a nation that was being sent sub-standard wheat by a rich country. His moral compass made a strong economic sense as he focused the country's attention toward agriculture and farming and initiated the Amul milk cooperative movement and the green revolution. He turned a crisis into an opportunity.

The so-called moral compass is a part of human cognition, and when that compass comes into action through human behavior, it turns an ordinary biological creature into a unique moral being of conscience. As Mr Azim Premji, chairman of Wipro, India's biggest corporate donor toward charity, explains that this ethical behavior is the cornerstone of corporate longevity, conscience instantly becomes a tangible, living, breathing thing.

Ethical dilemmas – How you respond is who you are

I often hear a lot about corporate vision, values, principles and the like. But let me be honest, more often than not, these patronizing statements from every organization sound pretty much similar and employees find those difficult to relate to. I have, in my career, followed a time-tested simple formula as the bedrock of the value system. It is based on the principle of doing the right things vs. doing things right, and it has worked for me.

Several times in my career, I had been faced with situations to act according to the process or do things that I felt were morally right but weren't always as per corporate guidelines. Whether it was to allow a colleague to work long term from home to take care of her ailing child or sheltering someone from organizational restructuring, I have gone against policies. Looking back, those decisions have in the long run helped the organization in earning invaluable employee loyalty. Ericsson has been winning the 'great place to work for' recognition for the last five consecutive years. I think a lot of this has to do with the way we have treated our people fairly and with respect.

The question can be: Am I guilty of doing charity at the company's expenses? I leave that to my readers to judge and ask themselves what they would have done as leaders. A pilot at Southwest Airlines went against policy and held a flight so that a passenger could reach the hospital in time to say goodbye to his dying grandson. While other airlines might have disciplined the pilot for his actions, the CEO of Southwest called the pilot to thank him for living the company's values.

The pilot's actions generated massive amounts of goodwill and shone a very public spotlight on Southwest's dedication to customer service. The pilot was asking himself a simple question: Who do I really work for? To him, the answer was, 'for the customer', in this case, the passengers. It helped him align corporate goals with his conscience. His decision was authentic leadership in action. Every organization talks about being customer-centric but only rarely do we find enterprises walking the talk. It is up to the leadership to show that they can indeed walk the talk.

One doesn't need to look far for inspirational leadership based on being authentic, ethical and guided by a strong moral compass. JRD Tata started Tata Airlines in 1932 along with an English friend, Neville Vincent. The Tatas and Neville had an agreement whereby Neville would get one-third of the profits. All the investments and the services of JRD came from the Tatas. In the first year of operation, the profit was Rs 60,000, which by today's value would be several hundred times more. By the time the contract expired five years later in 1937, the profit has multiplied ten times! JRD was no longer the Tata Chairman; J. D. Choksi, the legal advisor of the Tatas, thought the terms of the contract with Neville should be revisited as profits were much higher now.

JRD was not happy but went and told Neville so. Neville was terribly upset. Deep down, JRD was always aware that redrawing the contract would be unfair on the man who had first approached him with the idea and collaborated in implementing it. He consulted another legal expert, Dinshaw Daji, who was also a personal friend. Daji opined that while Choksi was legally correct, morally, he would not want to agree with it. JRD recounted later, "I went and told Neville, 'forget it', and assured him that the terms would be the same as before."

Organizations and individuals – whether they are leaders, managers or employees – often face such ethical dilemmas in their life and work and it is our responses to such situations that define who we are.

Just weeks after Sallie Krawcheck took over running Merrill Lynch's wealth management division, in the fall of 2009, she was told that the Stable Value Fund, a financial product Merrill had sold in 401k plans, wasn't actually so stable and had lost most of its value. Even worse, the people who would suffer most were low-income earners who had invested in the funds as part of their retirement savings plans – specifically, Walmart employees.

There were two options – either tell investors that it was plain bad luck or put more money into the fund and increase the value. Krawcheck did what she felt was right and put more money in, after convincing management that it was the right thing to do. She later said, "My indicator was my stomach. When my stomach hurts, I know something is wrong." She did not get fired.

Sometimes, we are tempted to avoid the tougher route of doing the right things because we think it would have an adverse financial impact on the organization or us as individuals. On countless occasions, I have found that to be a completely wrong notion. On the contrary, behaving with integrity is actually good business sense.

The Dove campaign is a wonderful example. Stacie Bright, their marketing director, was facing a moral dilemma in 2006. Dove had always used the traditional promotional approach with female models considered to be 'beautiful' in popular perception. But Bright was pained to find that these ads adversely affected her own daughter's self-esteem. She realized that such distress must be happening to all young girls with 'average' looks, who were exposed to this advertising.

Quitting was an option, but Bright decided to try out an alternative first. She designed a mock-up advert using photos of the daughters of all Dove directors. The text accompanying each photo was the girls' own words, explaining how they thought themselves to be not beautiful. Bright and her team showed it to the executives, confident that this was a risky but worthwhile move.

The risk worked. The company directors were deeply moved and immediately decided to reformulate Dove's marketing strategy, focusing more on 'natural beauty'. Dove doubled its profits from £1bn to £2bn and turned the business of selling soaps into a moral campaign. This campaign continues to date and has turned into a signature identity for Dove.

Data shows that ethical organizations do earn a premium for ethically doing business. Research from Ethisphere, which ranks the world's most ethical companies every year, shows that those who make it to the ethical list are valued higher than other companies. Leaders will be constantly faced with the development paradox – the more a country develops, the more natural resources it uses and the more it contributes toward the climate crisis.

The massive processing powers in our data centers that run cloud services make our businesses efficient and cost-effective. But the heat generated from these super-powerful computers and the cooling required to keep them humming along adds to global warming. Once again, our moral compass will have to work overtime to figure out the path we need to take. What else could we do to neutralize the environmental danger? This should be answered first before investing in such initiatives.

Indeed, if we are really smart thinkers, we can turn these paradoxes into opportunities. The successful businesses of tomorrow will be those that solve social problems, like climate change, drinking water shortage, increasing farm productivity via agro-tech, education, healthcare and so on. The moral compass can create incredible business value through innovating sustainable solutions. The internet of things, near zero-latency 5G connections, edge computing and Data Science can create sustainable solutions that will solve many of these challenges and also reduce global warming.

Businesses in a sustainable world will provide solutions more than services. Collaboration with other businesses, governments and civil society groups would become commonplace and partnerships will underpin successful business ventures. The consumer now has a much stronger voice, and organizations have established channels to interact with and learn from them, rapidly adapting their products based on demand. In turn, consumers, employees and shareholders will respect and reward such organizations.

Ethics, which are the foundation stone of individual and organizational values, have become increasingly important in a connected world where technology is transforming our lives and businesses at an unprecedented velocity. Organizations must rethink the old ways of doing business, which has been depleting the planet's natural resources. The biggest threat to organizations comes from internal sources from poor ethical standards.

The Take-Make-Dispose model must be replaced with Take-Make-Reuse, which needs leaders with a moral compass who think beyond quarterly results and bottom-line. In fact, it is the triple-bottom-line of People-Planet-Profits, which goes beyond financial measures of corporate success, which will become the value statement for every organization. It will call upon us to do the right things instead of always doing things right!

The business value of the moral compass will become indispensable in this age when advances in Artificial Intelligence (AI) will frequently create ethical dilemmas or issues of privacy vs. profits or figuring out who is responsible if a machine running on AI makes a mistake. When highly sophisticated machine learning systems are used to make significant decisions, it may be difficult to unravel the causes behind a specific course of action.

Machine learning systems can also be biased or reflect the biases of their trainers, in which case, leaders and managers of tomorrow must ensure it is non-discriminatory. In the future, machines might decide who can be a probable criminal or a likely loan defaulter. Relying only on machine intelligence can be profitable or efficient, but is it the right thing to do in every situation? This is a question that will keep haunting us.

Like any technology, AI will have dual uses and definitely pose ethical dilemmas. The same facial recognition technology can be used to find lost children or conduct civilian surveillance with evil political intentions. It is not the technology so much that dictates the moral dilemma as the human use case involved with the application, which makes the ethics of decision-making very difficult. Organizations will have to consider not just the ethical aspects of emerging technologies but also their possible use cases. Indeed, here we have an interesting opportunity to explore AI ethics because progress in AI technology would invariably lead to situations involving ethical dilemmas. Having in-depth knowledge of those issues is important for AI development. All these will need leaders to walk the path of doing the right things.

Our values and principles will be tested all the time and will bring us to the issue of authentic leadership. While ethical leadership focuses on compliance with external expectations, authentic leadership is about a leader's self-awareness, self-regulation and modeling these characteristics to subordinates. Each of us must find out the lodestar that makes our individual moral compasses work.

For organizations, the challenges are going to become even tougher as the global regulatory environment becomes more stringent. A new role of ethicists has evolved at the board level to ensure that ethics are taken seriously and embedded into decisions, products and services. In the future, we shall see the evolution of the bullet list of our organizational values becoming far more tangible in the form of ethical products.

Consumers, stakeholders, governments and capital markets will measure organizations on their ethics index. It will become unavoidable, and in such a scenario, those who have developed a strong DNA of doing the right things will emerge as winners. This will call for a different kind of leadership focused on delivering social value, and unless the moral compass is working, they will not be able to align corporate, individual and team goals with social objectives – that will be the leadership of the future. It will call on each of us to rise above ourselves and our narrow needs and ambitions to find the true purpose of our work. How can we connect what we are doing with the larger vision? Doing the right thing doesn't automatically bring success, but doing the wrong thing will almost certainly lead to failure!

Chapter 12

Being Always Right is Never Right

Let me present another paradox: If doing the right thing is the best option, then being always right is never right. Even if we think we're right, we must keep an option open to accept another point of view, which might be the right thing. Sounds confusing? Let me share an anecdote from my school days. There was a kid in my class in primary school, a very smart kid, who was ever ready to raise his hand whenever the teacher asked a question. The teachers liked him a lot. He was the kind of guy we have all encountered in our school days – the guy with all the answers, always right and never wrong. I don't know why but my close buddies and I didn't like him. Maybe he made us feel small and silly or like a bunch of kids who were plain idiots. He wasn't a bad guy at all, yet he irritated us with all the right answers. Or perhaps we were jealous of him.

Being always right is a very lonely path. When one is always right, others assume that the right person feels that they are wrong or that they don't know how to articulate the right answers. Over the years, in my career, I have constantly met people who are always right to such an extent that they appear to be without human failings. I had a colleague and a friend who had a brilliant mind when it came to technological issues. He was right most of the time. However, he always attempted to test out his ideas with others by starting with the sentence, 'I could be mistaken'.

That single opening sentence endeared him to others and encouraged them to come forth with their ideas, triggering a process of cross-pollination of myriad thoughts and suggestions. It was a highly creative process. I found in his style a fantastic method to create a consensus and, at the same time, an environment of knowledge sharing that eventually led to a far better idea than the one which we all started with.

I also had a colleague who had a unique way of looking at very complex technical issues. His mind enjoyed the intellectual challenge of finding answers to tough technological questions. However, he could get things wrong when presenting his ideas to the team by rubbishing all other suggestions.

Often, in times of great challenge, I have gathered my teams around me and told them that I needed their ideas to figure out a solution to a particularly tough situation. The effect it had on teams was fascinating. Everyone would begin to think, analyze the problem and address the solutions their own way and collectively at the same time. I found myself in the eye of an exciting tornado of ideas, at the end of which we usually found the answer to what we were looking for. It took the pressure off me to provide the answer to every problem. I didn't have to prove anything. I made everyone feel and be strong by recognizing their worth in the room.

One needs two things to encourage such a process – to listen with an open mind and accept that you can be wrong. Once you have gathered the ideas and arrived at some sort of thought about the right course of action, then it is your call to take over the action and lead. As they say, listen as if you are never right and lead as if you are always right.

Being a good listener won't just win you more friends, but it will sharpen your ideas with inputs from others. Sometimes, even if you listen intently, you might not be able to change a person's stand. But at least you will understand why someone is thinking the way they are. It helps one to figure out the positions that others might take in a situation.

It isn't enough to listen with an open mind, but it is vital to acknowledge the ideas of others, which has helped to refine your own. This is a process of getting others to contribute to the win and making it a collective victory, instead of an individual triumph. I had a friend at school who I realized that though he could have scored a goal, passed the ball to me to tap into the net. I was having a bad day in the field, and he just did it to make me feel happy and part of the success. The lesson left an indelible mark on me.

In football terms, this noble act is known as an 'assist'. This is one of the reasons why the Argentine star, Lionel Messi, ranks as one of the most selfless players in the game. Messi has 306 assists for his club and country. There is a lot of humility, grace and dignity in letting others share the glory, instead of taking it all even when the opportunity is there. Such actions cement the team with the most vital element of all human relationships – trust.

Trust is also one of the most essential forms of capital a leader and every team member have. Trust-building is an exercise that often requires considering totally new leadership perspectives. Leadership has conventionally been a story that was all about yourself – your vision and strategy, your ability to make the tough calls and rally the troops, your talents, your charisma and your heroic moments of courage and instinct. But leadership really isn't about you. It's more about empowering your team and your people through your presence and guidance and making sure that your leadership continues to impact them even when you are gone.

That's the fundamental principle we've learned in the course of dedicating our careers to making leaders and organizations better. As a leader, your job is to create conditions that would facilitate your people to utilize their potential to the fullest. And that's true not only when you're in the trenches with them but also when you're not around and even – this is the cleanest test – when you've permanently moved on from the team. We call it empowerment leadership. The more trust you build, the more easily can you put this kind of leadership to practice.

Getting yourself into accepting that you can be fallible and seeking ideas from others prevents us from falling prey to self-deception when we become immune to facts. Studies have shown that leaders are most likely to suffer from 'confirmation bias' or 'error blindness', where they filter out information that challenges their beliefs or ideas and accept those that are more supportive. This leads to mistakes, and often, it is too late to correct it. Being brave enough to admit you don't know everything protects your reputation. Trying to win every argument can risk your credibility.

The higher one climbs in the corporate hierarchy, the fatter the pay packet becomes. This is a natural process of being rewarded for your achievements. But this can also lead to a distorted view of reality and gives leaders the feeling of being infallible because of their higher compensation. Research by the University of Cambridge says that high-pay-induced CEO overconfidence leads to shareholder wealth losses from daring activities, such as overinvestment and value-destroying mergers and acquisitions. A higher pay makes leaders believe they're always right and that's why they are paid so much. It unconsciously clouds their judgment. They become overconfident on their plans and ideas. They tend to rationalize anything that supports their existing beliefs or ideas and rejects those that question their judgment.

My experience has been that this research is partly true as there is certain overconfidence that creeps in with success. It leads one to believe that he or she cannot be wrong if they have reached a certain position on the corporate totem pole. This is a critical time when one is seduced into shutting off ideas and thinking that one knows best. The leader is actually at his most vulnerable at this point, which is why we see CEOs and corporate lifespans shrinking. Credit Suisse has shown that the average age of a company listed on the S&P 500 fell from almost 60 years in the 1950s to less than 20 years in 2019. There are of course several reasons behind this, but an important one is the pressure that CEOs take upon themselves to be always right. Sometimes, I think we have forgotten to be wrong.

It is accepted that by being okay with being wrong, you keep your mind open. You pay greater attention to facts, instead of merely trying to win every argument and incorrectly focusing on what will help you defeat others. Andy Grove, Intel's co-founder, described this approach as the courage and confidence to act on what you know right now, along with the humility to course correct when new information comes along. You are not supposed to know it all. Wise leaders ask the right questions, not perfect answers. They nudge and inspire their teams to find new solutions. Also, leaders who acknowledge their limitations are less likely to make mistakes that put their teams and organizations in danger. On the other hand, some leaders believe that all failures are due to external factors and they are personally responsible for all successes.

Rather surprisingly, one sees these days that leaders of major global organizations are reluctant to admit their mistakes. In the recent past, we have seen how dominant social media enterprises, who have been careless about the way their user data have been misused and abused, refusing to outright admit to their errors. Instead, they sought recourse to legal languages, evading a complete apology. The more we continue to refuse to admit to our failings, the more we will see government regulations come down heavily. The choice is to either self-regulate, admit errors and correct or get corrected and face punitive actions.

Compare this to how Toyota, the Japanese car maker, handled its biggest nightmare that happened in 2010 when more than eight million cars were recalled and nearly 90 people were killed because of accidents caused by the defects. The CEO offered personal condolences to the families and emotionally apologized to all customers. To make sure everyone got the message, Toyota created an ad campaign, admitting it hadn't lived up to its safety standards and took out ads in major newspapers about how it would fix the safety issues. Mistakes will happen, whether at an organizational or an individual level. Leadership is about handling these mistakes and errors with humility, honesty and then moving on, rather than trying to hide them. Some organizations have done it with great dignity.

It was the mistake telecast live around the world – the wrong movie being announced as the Best Picture winner at the 2017 Oscars! PwC was the organization responsible for this blunder. The Academy of Motion Picture Arts and Sciences traditionally entrusted them with the task of counting the votes. Admirably, PwC made no excuses, acknowledged the mistake and tendered a crisp apology. The statement briefly explained what happened, apologized to the people involved and was gracious in thanking the people who handled the situation. Instead of allowing the embarrassment to linger, the way PwC owned responsibility, expressed their regrets and settled the issue once and for all was commendable. The firm had been performing this task of handing over the envelopes with the winners' names on those for 82 flawless years before this mistake took a huge toll on their brand.

In contrast, some organizations often choose to downplay their mistakes, which turn out to be major disasters later on. In April 2010, when a huge explosion in an oil rig owned by a petrochemical major spilled millions of gallons of oil into the Gulf of Mexico, the CEO of the firm described it as 'relatively tiny' compared to the 'very big ocean'. The explosion had killed 11 people and cost the company more than $40 billion in damages. Three months later, the CEO was out of a job. This was a case of a highly paid CEO who felt he was above criticisms and lost his humility.

Leaders who failed to keep an open mind and listen to others often do a great disservice to their organizations. Edgar F. Codd, an English Computer Scientist, invented the relational database for database management while employed with the world's foremost technology company. His invention served as the theoretical basis for all future relational databases and Relational Database Management Systems. While Codd's organization dithered on the idea, Larry Ellison and Oracle Corporation stepped into the picture. Oracle had just begun as a startup in Silicon Valley and needed a blockbuster product to really take off. Taking Inspiration from Codd's paper they developed their own database and brought it to the market, even before Codd's company could launch a product of their own.

Having learned watching several such missed opportunities during my career in every organization that I worked for, I have developed a process for listening, sorting, acting or parking ideas for action. No idea in my opinion, even if some of those sound ridiculous today, should be discarded outright without proper evaluation.

On several occasions, my ideas have met with severe opposition, cynicism, outright criticism and rejections. There can be two courses of action in such situations – fight doggedly for your ideas or step aside and let others take over. Over the years, I figured out that it is not necessary to win in every situation.

Chapter 13

Three Transformations, Three Journeys

Life doesn't always give us the luxury of choice. Things happen, and our well-planned world goes crazy. All the strategies we had so carefully worked out are suddenly redundant. A Black Swan event, like the COVID-19 pandemic, has made us all hit the pause button. We are faced with an existential question of lives vs. livelihoods. It suddenly struck me that this wasn't the first time it has happened to me. I have always lived through it, battled my way out of it and thankfully, survived and stayed relevant.

Most of the time, in life, we don't see a crisis barreling toward us. It's always a bolt out of the blue that, funnily enough, strikes when things just couldn't be better. The other thing about these sudden shocks is that they're triggered by apparently unconnected events but somehow, the dots are connected. It is perhaps the much-debated butterfly effect, where a butterfly flaps its wings in Boston and stirs up a tornado in Tokyo. My world in Kolkata, India, went topsy-turvy by the events happening nearly 9000 miles away in another continent in Houston, Texas, US. However, topsy-turvy isn't always such a bad deal, as I discovered later. There's always an opportunity lurking in what at first appears to be an obstacle – that was a big learning.

It was a mild winter evening on December 2, 2001, in Kolkata, when news broke in fits and starts over a lethargic few-kbps nascent internet connection that one of the world's biggest energy company, Enron, based in Houston, had filed for Chapter 11 under US bankruptcy laws, declaring itself insolvent.

This corporate event apparently had little to do with me, a young man in my twenties, tasked with setting up the SAP delivery practice out of India for PricewaterhouseCoopers, which was then one of the leading big-five consulting and auditing services firm. SAP was a global leader in packaged ERP (Enterprise Resource Planning) products and services. Dramatically, Enron changed the course of my personal journey. It led me to one of the most incredibly exciting phases of my life.

ERP was the technology rage in the nineties. When PwC started its IT services business, we, from India, were leading the charge. The big challenge for us was to create an IT services and technology consulting practice in a firm that has traditionally been known for its audit and taxation services. IT was something that firms like PwC didn't venture into. We were breaking new grounds and doing a fabulous job of it. So much so that technology service revenues had begun to outstrip the traditional audit services.

Just when our IT advisory and implementation practice was poised to scale greater heights, the Enron scandal turned everything chaotic, and my life was transformed yet again. While Enron had collapsed under a massive financial scandal, it also brought down Arthur Anderson (AA), one of the largest of the big-five audit and consulting firms. AA was the auditor of Enron and provided the energy company with consulting services. The firm was held responsible by the US authorities for failing to raise alerts over its client's financial wrongdoings.

The US Congress, in a sharp response to the scandal, passed the Sarbanes Oxley Act in 2002, which required audit firms to disassociate their consulting business from the audit practice. AA was dissolved in 2002 when the firm voluntarily surrendered its licenses to practice as Certified Public Accountants in the US. The lawmakers felt that as the consulting business was more lucrative compared to audit, big-five firms were allegedly compromising on an audit to bag more profitable consulting businesses from the same client. The Enron scandal singed PricewaterhouseCoopers as well, which had to comply with the Sarbanes Oxley Act. In October 2002, the consulting business was carved out and sold to IBM. My world changed forever.

Along with about 2000 of my PwC colleagues in India, we joined IBM as the first batch of IT consulting professionals. We were to set up Big Blue's IT offshoring beachhead in India and be the arrowhead for the technology services operations to meet its internal and client requirements. This was the genesis of IBM's transformation from a hardware organization to a software and services company.

I decided to join IBM as I felt that it was a fantastic prospect to create something that had never been done before. Imagine being hired with the others to transform the iconic IBM! It was far too tempting a learning opportunity to give up. There was a larger purpose that called me.

I had felt the same excitement in my heart when, in the early nineties, I joined Price Waterhouse (PW), as it used to be called before its merger with Coopers & Lybrand in 1998. Price Waterhouse, during that time, was building its technology services and offshoring business. PW had changed my life when from a very small company, SQL Star, I was recruited overnight by the consulting firm. SQL Star was one of the many vendors selected for implementing an ERP project by Tribeni Tissues, a specialized paper manufacturing company headquartered in Kolkata. The project was being managed overall by PW. I was responsible for designing four SAP financial modules of the project and worked closely with the Chief Financial Officer of the client. He took a keen interest in my work and was delighted with what I was delivering for his company. But I wasn't too pleased with the way things were being managed and decided to quit.

My decision to quit had created a project risk, and the client wanted to mitigate it by influencing PW to hire me to avoid disrupting the work. On Diwali day, I resigned from SQL Star and joined another company in the morning. By the same afternoon, I received a call from the leader of the technology practice of PW, followed by a very short meeting for a few minutes. By the evening, I resigned again to join PW.

Only a few days before this, I was initially rejected by the PW human resources executive, who felt I wasn't quite cut out for a blue-blooded consulting firm that hired its talent from the IIMs, IITs and the US Ivy League institutions. I don't really blame him for disqualifying me. I had too many rough edges. My English communication was rudimentary, and I perhaps lacked the sophistication of classical consultants who spoke with a clipped accent and knew the perfect business attire for the occasion.

This would not be the first time I would face, if you may call it so, subtle discrimination for not fitting stereotypes. In IBM too, I was assessed initially as not having in me the qualities of a true blue IBM-er, which eventually led the company to assign a mentor for me. My new mentor realized that I would get the job done in the organization even though I wasn't a typical dyed-in-the-wool Big Blue person and very graciously offered to teach me the IBM ways of working. I gained enormously from this relationship and personal connection, and we struck a great professional rapport. This person was a very senior executive reporting to the CEO. It helped me to realize the tremendous pressures of leadership and even the physical strength needed to handle it.

IBM was a fascinating experience of working with a great team in turning around a huge ocean liner at the speed of a jet ski. A monolithic iconic organization has well-established processes honed over the years, which then appeared to me like inexplicable roadblocks designed to slow things down exactly when we needed blazing fast responses. And yet the 2000-strong forward force grew the IT business to nearly 45,000 people in India. IBM's IT services and technology consulting practice soon overshadowed its hardware business. Today, IBM is more of a software and services company than a hardware organization.

It was a landmark achievement for all of us in the team. I still remember the founder of one of India's leading IT service company that was based in Bangalore, boast about how, now that the Big Blue had dared to step onto its home turf in India, they would slaughter it. IBM went on to win not only major global contracts on the strength of its India operations but also became a force to reckon within the country. Clients had said that whoever decided to hire IBM for its services wouldn't get fired. I took the battle right to the gates of the home-grown technology companies.

I hired dozens of trucks and created mobile advertising platforms out of those. The communication team created huge billboard signs that simply stated 'IBM is Hiring' and mounted them on the trucks! Those vehicles were parked right outside the offices of the technology companies in the electronic city in Bangalore, outside college gates. Soon, we were flooded with applications to recruit and build our teams. I have deep respect for our local India-born MNCs, who have proved the country's capabilities to the rest of the world, but I had a vision to fulfill.

Big Blue, with its daunting bureaucratic structure, awe-inspiring technology prowess and world-leading intellectual capabilities was an experience that was worth a few university degrees. Coming from PwC, where we started the technology practice from scratch and were reasonably empowered to take swift decisions, IBM looked intimidating from within. It taught me how large global organizations, employing hundreds of thousands of people present in every continent in almost 170 countries operated.

Let me be candid in admitting that I was utterly frustrated when what I considered logical requests to grow the business were being turned down by someone in Apac (Asia-Pacific). It was my sheer doggedness of not giving up that got things moving. To give an example, a request to allocate seats to people we had hired got approved only after the third time it was made to some faceless person in another part of the world. I felt as if my requests for infrastructure to make people productive were being made to a wall. Only later, after meeting that faceless person, the regional CFO, did I understand his reasons behind rejecting my requests.

What he told me was a lesson in running mega-corporations. His department received requests that would need investments of over US$1 billion if all of them were to be approved and would perhaps drive the company toward bankruptcy. They were designed to reject requests for the first few times, just to test the tenacity of the person making the request. The logic is that if the requestor believed in it earnestly, they would have a solid business case and would keep at it, and eventually, it would get approved.

According to the regional CFO, about 70% of the requestors did not follow up after the first rejection and most gave up after the second time their request was rejected. Only the few who pursued got a proper review of their business case after which investments would be sanctioned. They tested who had a purpose larger than just a 'good to have' kind of request, maybe just to get additional hiring tickets for expanding their own sphere of influence. This process was their way of figuring out which proposals met the organization's overarching objectives.

It was at that point in time that it dawned on me that one of the biggest issues faced by global enterprises was the complexity of size, extremely large organizations spread across several countries, spanning continents, straddling diverse cultures, grappling with local and global regulations at the same time. What worked in one country took time in another part of the world or even got rejected.

In Ericsson – an organization that will celebrate its 150th birthday in a few years from now and is present in 180 countries – the environment was quite different. It was a highly democratic and consensus-driven organization where it was important to get everyone on board for most major decisions. Initially, it appears exasperating as things get slowed down when speed is the essence of competitiveness, more so for an organization that was late in the captive offshoring business.

The fast decision of pushing empowerment down to the lowest levels was critical for Ericsson in 2010 when it started its captive unit in India – Ericsson Global Services India. The Swedish giant was battling to stay ahead in the race as aggressive Chinese players, who were supported by their government with limitless access to funds and were disrupting the business.

The organization enjoyed the absolute trust of its global telecom clients when it came to hardware, but it lacked an important piece of the puzzle – services. It had to quickly get its act together to create new competencies around services and generate fresh streams of revenues that were on the table but were being picked up by IT service providers.

As I was settling down for dinner one evening, my former boss and friend in IBM, who had left the company to join Ericsson in Sweden, called me up. He asked if I would be interested in creating another India offshoring story. My first reaction was utter bewilderment. I had no knowledge of telecom, and he was asking me to venture into a completely unknown technology terrain. We debated and discussed, and finally, I made up my mind not to take up his offer. However, for old times' sake, I took the trip to Sweden on Ericsson's invitation to meet the then CEO and CFO.

I heard him out about their plans for India and how it was to transform Ericsson. I opened the discussion with an honest confession that my only experience in telecom was using a mobile phone for the last 15 years and that didn't qualify me for the job. They said that was exactly why they wanted someone like me. Ericsson had enough telecom professionals but few who knew IT and offshoring. I didn't have a counter-argument and flew back to India with the offer to join this iconic Swedish enterprise.

Ericsson turned out to be even more exciting than my previous experiences. From just 1500 people, we grew the organization to over 23,000 in four quick years that went by like a twinkling of the eye. Looking back today, the beginning was a challenging task to get what was then a 140-year-old organization to sprint like a teenager. We were competing against Indian IT service companies, who not only offered the most competitive rates but were also agile in the marketplace. In comparison, Ericsson appeared to take longer to respond to the needs. Internal processes, too, were complex and consumed a lot of management time to maneuver. This caused the usual frustration among people who had come from different organizations with a much faster pace of doing things.

My efforts were mostly to reason with the team to make them understand the culture of the new organization, its ways of doing things, the processes and people and respect the legacy of this institution that had revolutionized telecommunication through the ages. It was a company that began life in the industrial age and moved through the age of electricity and was now readying itself to play a vital role in the digital revolution.

In all these years, the company had continuously transformed itself from a telegraph repair shop in Stockholm in 1876 to making the first 500-point automatic switching equipment, the first digital telephone exchange, the innovator of Erlang, the open-source language, the LTE and Bluetooth. Ericsson designed the first version of Erlang in the 1980s, and it has been available as open-source since then. Today, it is adopted for developing applications in the banking, e-commerce and online gaming sectors among others, while the user community continues to grow. Even WhatsApp used Erlang.

Once this respect for history was there, the task of aligning people to the grand vision of building a new Ericsson ready for the Fourth Industrial Revolution became smoother. It was my IBM experience that helped me figure out why it took such a long time for the organization to respond and make decisions, apparently oblivious to the need for speed. I spent a year in Stockholm, the headquarters of this Swedish company, which has a repository of 54000 patents as of date and had spearheaded the telecom revolution in every decade since its existence.

A small incident helped me understand how this huge organization worked. Ericsson has a convention for naming products, projects, services or even business units. Every proposed name has to be validated by this team that checked whether the suggested name was offensive in any language or meant something else other than its intended purpose. Every name must pass the cultural sensitivity test of 170 countries. This takes time. What looked like a needless bureaucratic bottleneck was actually protecting the organization from possible damaging litigations or hurting the sentiments of someone in a distant country. The brand was built with so much care over the years by people who have worked for generations in the organization. It was far too precious to be exposed to such vulnerabilities.

What I learned in all these transformation journeys of centurion organizations is that while the leadership understood the challenges the respective organizations faced, the management layers below them took a while to get on the same strategy wavelength and execute the plans. This happens for two reasons. First, most leadership communication lacks clarity and the 'why' of the strategic decision is not communicated clearly. The second is the perceived threat to existing roles and responsibilities as the organization makes this huge pivot.

In every instance, it boils down to communication gaps leading to insecurity about jobs, loss of seniority and being rendered irrelevant in the new way of doing things. There is no dearth of intent, sincerity and purpose. It is the communication cobwebs that at times delayed or distorted the messages. 'Get the messages right, explain the why and keep on communicating' is my mantra that differentiates why some organizations are successful and some are not. If the why is explained, then people will figure out the how and achieve the objectives.

A third and perhaps the most important reason why such strategic directions take a long time to yield desired benefits is cultural conflicts. The new recruits, in the case of my first transformation experience in PwC, were from an entirely different educational background from the existing leadership. They were mostly young engineers belonging to a new generation of Indians willing to win the world and challenge long-held ideas and thoughts, while the existing employees and leadership were steeped in tradition and dyed-in-the-wool auditors. The contrast was as sharp as between collarless T-shirts paired with sneakers and pinstriped suits combined with ties and matching socks.

In my second experience of being in the thick of a transformation journey at IBM, the new set of employees from a consulting firm were confident about their knowledge of selling services-based projects and how things were done. Most importantly, they had carved out a niche for themselves in a highly traditional environment with their easy-going but professional attitude. They had dismantled bureaucracy and got things done fast to successfully compete with a new set of IT service players who were highly agile and nimble.

This group of people met with an organization that appeared frighteningly bureaucratic from the inside. The ways of working were governed by a set of rules and processes that didn't meet the competitive requirements of the new world of IT services and offshoring. The cultural conflict became a serious post-merger issue as the salespeople who were used to dealing with hardware were at a loss trying to sell IT services. And those selling IT services thought it beneath themselves to sell hardware or 'boxes' as they derogatively described the servers and laptops. They were used to selling and implementing software-based solutions.

Most importantly, companies like IBM or Ericsson were competing with far more nimble Indian companies that were quick to make decisions and respond to client requests. They operated in another extreme, where getting more business came before adhering to processes. Also, there was a lot of empowerment in these home-grown organizations, which wasn't the case in typical global MNCs that operated along defined lines of command and control.

However, due credit must be given to the leadership of such organizations that they realized that drastic changes – in the way in which things were being run – was urgent and took steps to make those happen without compromising on compliance and control. This is a hallmark of great leadership that foreknows the need for transformation and is proactive about it.

The case of Ericsson was almost similar. The salesforce that had been selling equipment now had to learn about ICT services and often found the transition challenging. To put yourself in the shoes of the existing long-term employees, it was difficult to accept that telecom hardware had become commoditized and that the differentiation now lay in services. The competitive landscape they were used to had changed. At the same time, I also realized that success depends on quick course corrections, which these large organizations are quite capable of when challenged.

Ericsson, today, is realigning itself with its customer needs. According to analysts, when many communications service providers (SPs) are entering the strategic planning phase related to 5G, edge computing and IoT, Ericsson's overarching goal has been clearly defined to enable its communications SP customer base to drive new revenue streams.

Ericsson has quickly reversed course from its M&A-driven expansion into media, shuttered its industry and society or verticals-focused business and relaunched itself as a 'communications SP enabler', providing industry-leading solutions around radio, mobile core, OSS/BSS and services. This course-shifting initiated by the leadership is deliberate as it seeks to not only improve profitability in all business lines but also cement its standing among telco stakeholders ready to select 5G partners for the next decade.

Organizations like Ericsson or IBM are constantly rediscovering their competitive advantage. This is where I learned the true meaning of the saying, 'what got you here, won't get you there'. They are always thinking of what's next and everyone knows that next is now. It wasn't enough for organizations to realize this truth at the leadership levels only. It needed to be effectively communicated to the rest of the organization. The communication was persistent, regular and constantly reinforcing the messages. There is nothing called 'over-communication'. This is what separates the winners and losers – the ability of the leadership to motivate its people and align their personal aspirations with organizational goals. I have always found that this simple formula of giving people the why and letting them work out the how always works.

This is the same for individuals. Those who find a larger purpose in their work are always more successful than those who take a narrower view of what it means to their careers only. We all know that famous story where President Kennedy visiting the NASA premises for the first time asks a janitor with a broom what he does there, and the man proudly replies, "I'm helping put a man on the moon!" One will always need to take a panoramic view of the world we live in, the organization we work for, the businesses we create, find the larger purpose and then connect the dots. That is the secret of success.

I have always been grappling with questions like why some leaders are successful and some others are not. What is leadership about? Why are some employees highly motivated while others are not? Why do some people fail while others don't find success although they work hard? Like the opportunity masquerading in the shape of a crisis swept me up in its tide, the larger purpose of what we do and what makes us successful struck me like lightning, some 6500 kilometers away from my hometown, during a visit to Africa.

Ever since I had taken my kids to watch the Disney movie, *Lion King*, and walked away fascinated by the wildlife, Africa was on my bucket list. I went on a holiday to that continent a few years back. Like any tourist, I visited Maasai Mara, in south-western Kenya, to be up close with nature and wildlife. I had even bought a long lens for my camera to take close-ups of the animals. As I was getting close, I could see a spectacular sight of an incredible variety of animals – rhinos, elephants, giraffes, wildebeests, zebras and gazelles – moving through the Maasai Mara ecosystem. All of them were living together in the same space.

As I wondered how amazing it was to see those animals coexist, I was rudely brought down to reality when a beautiful baby gazelle was casually chased, hunted down and devoured by a cheetah. It shared the kill with its cubs. Next, I witnessed how a pride of lions stalked and killed zebras as a team and how hyenas kill baby deer. It made me miserable and unhappy. It shattered my worldview of peaceful coexistence. I returned to the tent and started pondering over my bad decision of coming down all the way just to witness the brutal slaughter of small beautiful animals by cruel predators. We all see it on Discovery Channel but witnessing it firsthand appeared way more gruesome. The world looked unfair!

That evening, sitting listlessly among the campfire gathering, the answer came to me from the earthy African wisdom passed down generations since the dawn of time. Our guide explained how things worked. If you simply looked at the killing of these beautiful animals by the more powerful predators – the lions and cheetahs – you'd see only half the picture.

The other half was that this killing was essential; the very essence of the food chain. If the lions didn't kill the gazelles, one day, there would be too many of them. Then there would be a shortage of grazing land and the animals would raid farmlands and devour the crops. If they ate the crops, the humans would starve. The lions kept us, humans, alive. I remembered what Mufasa said in *Lion King*, "Everything you see exists together in a delicate balance. As king, you need to understand that balance and respect all the creatures, from the crawling ant to the leaping antelope."

There are symbiotic relationships in nature that work to the benefit of both species, playing a key role in their survival. Any time you see a herd of zebras in Africa, you are sure to find wildebeests close by. These two species work perfectly together. They both feed on grasses but the difference is in the types. While zebras eat tall grass, the hordes of wildebeests devour the shorter variety. As they feed, the zebras clear away the tall growth, making way for the wildebeests to access the shorter type left behind.

The world will survive only when we, like the zebra and the wildebeest, learn to coexist. It is important to understand that not every piece of the puzzle will fall into place. In every business decision, there will be a risk to take. The world can only survive on collaboration and creating networks. We will have to learn to compete and cooperate at the same time.

These are some of the lessons I connected to my workplace. Suddenly, I realized the true meaning of purpose, which we completely miss at times. Sometimes, we get lost in detail, missing the wood for the trees. The understanding of the purpose and making others understand the same makes some leaders successful, keeps employees highly motivated and spurs people to achieve what they never thought they could.

People up the ladder have an advantage. They have a better understanding of the overall situation. I call it a panoramic view. The view from a vantage point is how I describe a panoramic view. When you can help everyone understand what role they play in the very wide landscape, by helping them connect the dots, you will get the most motivated workforce. Successful organizations and their leaders do it the best. Leaders are those who are able to give their people a larger purpose of the work they are doing. At times, the small tasks they are performing becomes so much more significant when viewed this way.

I used to watch young people staring intently at eight large screens in front of them in our Network Operations Center (NOC) at Ericsson. They are the people constantly watching how your telecom network is performing and triggering an alert if they notice something wrong, which could lead to a disruption in the connection. It can be a tiresome, thankless job and gets quite monotonous after a while.

Often, while visiting the NOCs, I asked people what they were doing. Most of them said that they were monitoring the networks. Their faces lit up, eyes sparkled and shoulders widened when I told them that they are actually saving lives, helping businesses run, driving the economy or perhaps changing the lives of someone in Africa, someone they won't ever meet in their lifetimes.

From my vantage point, I could see the context. I became a storyteller and shared my perspective with those youngsters in the NOC. Context helps. Mobile Payment in Uganda started in 2008. Some 25 million people use Mobile Money. Before Mobile Money, the farmers and shop owners had to go to the bank to deposit their cash once a week, traveling long distances. People used to get robbed and could not visit doctors with money. This solved their problem. When we built Mobile Money, our biggest motivation was helping people living safe, not just writing lines of C++ codes. That was the real purpose of our work.

My NOC team walked with a different attitude of confidence and pride that afternoon. They had evolved from a job mindset, which only looked how much they got paid to beyond a career mindset that associated work with power or influence measured in team-size or influence to elevate themselves to a higher purpose of delivering technology for human good.

Many years ago, I was traveling through Changi airport in Singapore and had a three-hour layover between connecting flights. Those days in the early 2000s, there was not much automation and human labor was still employed in keeping the airport clean. I noticed an elderly lady, who must have been in her seventies. Her skin was wrinkled. She shuffled more than she walked.

The lady held a bucket of cleansing liquid in one hand and a rubber wiper in the other. For nearly 45 minutes, I watched her clean a glass windowpane as if that was the most important job in the world. After she left it squeaky clean, I walked up to the window and, trust me, there wasn't even a speck on the pane. That must have been the cleanest window on the Earth. When the work was done, she stepped back and looked at the glass, like an artist admiring a painting. She allowed herself a quiet smile and gently moved to the next pane. Observing her, I learned what dedication meant. It's the difference between a job, a career and a purpose. This was what no management lesson could ever teach me.

Chapter 14

Thinking of Possibilities Critically

I was about to make the momentous decision to leave Pricewaterhouse Coopers and join IBM in 2002, which was taking over the IT consulting practice of the firm, along with a few of our colleagues. But like many others, I had more than enough reasons to stay back. I was a partner in a respected Big Four consulting firm and life was comfortable. IBM, on the other hand, was primarily a hardware company that was trying to foray into the consulting and IT services business. It would mean working with people I didn't know and being in a colossal organization where I would perhaps feel lost. While PwC offered a comfortable existence of the known, IBM was the big unknown. I would have to prove myself once again, working through its legendary bureaucracy and creating a services business that didn't exist in scale.

Some of my colleagues raised the topic to evaluate the options to stay back. In those tense days of the takeover, there was an unwritten left side and right side divide among the professionals of the firm. The left side represented those who would be staying back in the firm, and the right side was those who would move over to IBM. I was convinced that being on the right side was the right thing and even communicated that to quite a few of my colleagues who were caught in two minds.

My reasoning was simple: It was all about the possibilities of what we could do from within the world's largest technology company at that point in time. In PwC, we had created a global business that was now attractive enough to fetch nearly $3 billion – the price IBM was paying for the acquisition. To me, IBM represented new possibilities of what else we could do, building on the foundations of the technology behemoth. This enormous potential was what attracted me and overshadowed the anxieties of being in a new ecosystem.

An IBM press release on October 2, 2002, proudly proclaimed, "The combination creates a new global business unit, IBM Business Consulting Services, comprising more than 30,000 IBM and 30,000 transferring PwC Consulting professionals. As a result, IBM Business Consulting Services becomes the world's largest consulting services organization with operations in more than 160 countries." I was going to be a part of a 60,000-strong global consulting team. While some felt daunted, I was stirred by the amazing potential this merger offered.

Everything in me said this journey had to be embarked upon. This was the second time I was taking a different fork in the road. I had done it before in the early stages of my career when I took up the role of managing the project in Nepal, the success of which would help the entry of PwC into offshore IT consulting. Now, I decided to join the journey to transform Big Blue.

Out of the comfort zone

New shores were beckoning me. Ships, as they say, are not built to be in safe harbors but to be on the oceans. We were part of a team that was reinventing this company founded way back in 1911 that survived and thrived through three industrial revolutions. It also played a prominent role in a couple of these revolutions.

Others in India shared similar thoughts and came along for the ride. As expected, it wasn't an easy journey. Processes seemed byzantine, we appeared to be spending more time battling through innumerable regulations, rules and guidelines instead of creating new offerings for customers. All this was new to me and a huge learning, not without its share of frustrations.

One of the biggest surprises was the quarterly review meetings that we had in IBM – a practice that didn't exist in PwC. The consulting firm believed a lot in strategy, and strategies couldn't be evaluated quarterly. In one such review meeting, I presented my ideas on what we would do next quarter. This triggered a round of laughter in the conference room from true blue IBM-ers.

One of them quipped, "Amitabh, you're a visionary as you think about the next quarter. We think only about the current quarter."

My new learning was that we have two plans – a short-term plan to see us till the end of the day and a long-term plan to run till the end of the month! That kind of suited my mantra of taking each day at a time.

Working in IBM was not easy. It was steeped in tradition yet led to technological revolutions and offered amazing opportunities to those willing to grab it. However, it was a good thing that Ginni Rometty, who succeeded Sam Palmisano as the CEO of IBM and led the PwC acquisition, didn't believe in being comfortable.

During one of her many media interviews, Ginni said, "You have to learn to be comfortable with being uncomfortable or you won't grow. I often ask people, 'When do you feel you grew the most during your career?' They typically mention a time when they took a risk. Growth and comfort never coexist. If you're not nervous about something, it means you're not learning." Being uncomfortable opens opportunities and possibilities.

Think, question and disagree

Thinking about possibilities, potentials and different scenarios rather than looking at the immediate is what defines critical thinking, which is so important today. In this, we are aided by the huge amount of information available by technology that processes this information, turning it into actionable intelligence. But a lot depends on critical thinking, which is how our neurons process the hidden layers in obvious information and decide on the action to be taken. This is about using our judgment, something that machines still cannot do. It enables us to see patterns and question anything that doesn't fit this pattern, the outlier pieces of the puzzle. People with good judgment are skeptical of information that doesn't make sense.

None of us might be alive today if it weren't for a Soviet lieutenant colonel by the name of Stanislav Petrov. It came to light only after the fall of communism that one day in 1983, as the duty officer at the USSR's missile tracking center, Petrov was advised that Soviet satellites had detected a US missile attack on the Soviet Union. He decided that the 100% probability reading was implausibly high and so did not report the information upward, despite his instructions. Instead, he reported a system malfunction. "I had all the data [to suggest a missile attack was ongoing]," he told the BBC's Russian service in 2013. "If I had sent my report up the chain of command, nobody would have said a word against it." It turned out that the satellites had mistaken sunlight reflected from clouds for enemy missile engines. Petrov's inaction saved the world.

In a world where executive decisions will increasingly be data-driven, the criticality of human judgment will continue to be supreme. We will of course rely on data, but in the end, it would be our alert minds that will decide. This comes from training our minds to think critically, laterally taking a host of factors into account before deciding the final course of action. As machines would learn to perform most of our tasks, humans would need to focus on things that machines cannot do. It will be about seeing possibilities and opportunities where others don't or turning a situation around to create a solution.

Years ago, I heard this legend about how Bata (the shoe manufacturer) representatives saw an opportunity in a country where most people walked barefoot. Around the end of the nineteenth century, all shoe manufacturers in Victorian England sent representatives to that country to understand business prospects there. All of them returned with the same answer: "Nobody wears shoes there. So there is no market for our products there." All, except one, who came back and reported: "Nobody wears shoes. So there's a huge market for our products!"

Let us, for a moment, recall that anecdote where a man was driving a flock of sheep slowly down a country lane bounded by high banks. A motorist in a hurry came up behind the flock and urged the shepherd to move his sheep to the side so that the car could drive through. The shepherd refused since he could not be sure of keeping all the sheep out of the way of the car in such a narrow lane. Instead, he reversed the situation. He told the car to stop and then quietly turned the flock around and drove it back past the stationary car. The shepherd had instinctively thought through the possibilities and taken the most effective decision.

The best part of critical thinking is that it isn't a native skill but can be learned. According to the World Economic Forum's Future of Jobs report, skills like critical thinking and social intelligence will be more resistant to automation, which will eliminate 75 million jobs by 2025. This was a pre-COVID-19 forecast. I am sure that the figure will need to be revised upwards today.

I have my own way of questioning assumptions and taking nothing for granted. I continuously question my theories and get others to challenge me. Then I try to assess the logic behind the assumptions. If it's not logical, then it's probably incorrect and must be struck off the list. I look for evidence that supports the assumptions and test out the veracity of those. My decision to leave PwC for IBM was not a knee jerk reaction but a deliberate action derived from a careful assumption of the possibilities offered. I had discussed it threadbare with a few colleagues whose judgment I valued and then we made the decision. I tend to avoid jumping into conclusions.

Getting a team that is not afraid to challenge the status quo and ask questions is extremely important to test out our ideas. Companies like Toyota have turned this into a process that they call 'Pick a friendly fight'. There, employees offer constructive criticism without being worried about how they'll be viewed by their managers. It's the right thing to do if you want honest and frank insight.

I purposefully seek out people who aren't afraid to disagree with me. In turn, I am equally candid about disagreeing with my bosses whenever required. I believe that unless I do it, I am not thinking critically about decisions, the organization's future and our necessary actions. In short, I am not serving my organization honestly if I dare not to disagree. Remember, this kind of thinking leads us to become active members of our organizations, taking meaningful action to make the change we want to see.

An organization isn't something that happens to you. Rather, it is you who make choices every day that shape and make your organization into something of your own envisioning. Your company needs you and needs you to believe in a future that is better than the past and better than the present. Your company needs you to dream and engage. That's really what is at the heart of possibility thinking and expected from a truly engaged employee.

Chapter 15

The View from a Vantage Point

My trip to Maasai Mara during my trip to Africa was transformative in an intensely personal way. As I was getting close to the raw forces of nature, I had this feeling of gradually getting distant from my known world – from my workstation and my regular life in the city. It wasn't the kind of fleeting feeling you get every time you take a break and explore distant lands. It was more profound – an experience happening somewhere deep within, something intangible, indescribable yet very real.

When we reached Masai Mara, in south-western Kenya, we were just in time for the unfolding annual drama – one of the largest migrations of land mammals in the world. We had climbed a hilltop to observe this spectacular canvas of countless different kinds of animals – over two million wildebeest, zebras and gazelles – moving through the Serengeti and Maasai Mara ecosystems in search of green pastures. Even when seen through camera lenses and on television screens, this grand march for survival looks awe-inspiring. But viewed live from a vantage point, I simply did not have words to describe my feelings.

Studies using aerial photography show a remarkable level of organization in the structure of the wildebeest herds as they start moving. The groups display a wavy front that snakes out like the head of a swarm. This amazing structure cannot be apparent to each individual wildebeest, which means that there is some degree of decision-making happening between the animals.

I came back a changed person. I walked into my workstation, gazed around and realized the importance of using a reverse telescope to look at the issues before me. Once those were contextualized against the panoramic view, I could afford to take out the microscope to detail the execution plan. To understand the grand design, I need to zoom out first and then zoom in to address the minutiae.

This was transformative in the way we addressed problems. Instead of launching straight into execution, we looked at why was there a problem in the first place. I began to ponder, far more than ever before, over the questions to ask. I began to question the question itself. Is it the right question I'm asking? Is it the right problem we're trying to solve? As we delved deep and peeled through the layers of the challenges, the solutions presented themselves far more easily than before. Perception is all about getting your perspective right. Solutions appeared as if on its own when we spent the time to describe the right problem.

A perspective about perspectives

Some time ago, I read a fascinating book on spending a lot of time studying facts to analyze a problem and figuring out whether it was a real problem or not. We often spend hours and days, trying to find the right answers to wrong questions or solving the wrong question itself. I learned that building a large expensive hospital might not be a solution to the chronic problem of child mortality in India or Africa. Instead, a bar of soap to each member of the family in the affected regions would perhaps save more lives. This is what the panoramic view taught me – to look at the problem from a completely different perspective and find a solution to it.

The panoramic view also came with a mixed blessing. It wasn't enough to look at the problem from 50,000 feet above sea level to understand its interconnections with several other things – one also needed 5000-feet and 50-feet views of the issues. That provides better-rounded and closer-to-the-ground perspectives. Humanity is obsessed with how high we can go – space, unconquered peaks and the universe are challenges we cherish. Yet if we don't have the 50-feet view of the tactical issues, we will never be able to take concrete actions to execute the grand vision on a panoramic scale. Too high and you might suffer from altitude sickness; too low and you would fail to see the interconnections!

The Orbital Perspective

It was June 2008, and US astronaut, Ron Garan, was on a space walk outside the International Space Station orbiting the Earth every 90 minutes. He was floating some 250 kilometers above the Earth. For Ron, a former fighter pilot and a veteran astronaut, this was the fourth spacewalk of his career. But something incredible happened that day.

Looking at the Earth, it struck him like a flash of lightning that this stunning, fragile blue-green oasis on which we were born without a choice or option that has till now, protected all life from diverse cosmic hazards was full of appalling contradictions. Despite indescribable beauty, some inequities were destroying this paradise offered to us. He visualized the planet as a blue spaceship on which we were all astronauts traveling through space. He could see no borders that divided the human race. The realization hit him in the gut with a sobering effect. He termed it the Orbital Perspective.

Floating high above our planet, the orbital perspective enabled Ron to look at global problems through the lens of complete detachment. He found the answer to why our world still faces so many critical problems, regardless of the ample technology and resources we have at our disposal. It was only because we, humans, always fail to effectively collaborate on a global scale. With our feet grounded, we never see the whole. Ron saw the world from an angle that allowed him to visualize an interconnected and collaborative world without boundaries, where an exponential increase in technology made the impossible possible daily.

This cockpit or panoramic view helps us focus on the real issues facing humanity and our planet. What you knew or learned becomes a realization. For me, it was the comprehension that humans were inexorably connected with the floating mass of life before me at Masai Mara. All lives were interconnected, I realized. The planet needed the gazelle, the lion, the acacia trees and the green pastures, as much as it needs humanity. We all had a shared destiny. Ron returned to Earth and devoted himself to teaching people that the right order was 'planet, society and economy' and not the other way around.

Knowing myself

Many can effortlessly travel through these extreme altitudes to create value, not only for their organizations but also for the planet, looking at the big picture, zooming into tactical issues and directing execution toward the end-objective with effortless ease. However, the biggest challenge is understanding myself to start my transformation journey toward self-awareness. I need to know where I stand before I decide to move.

Watching the animals before me from my hilltop viewpoint, the interconnections in the circle of life became apparent. It was the beginning of a realization that was always there: The cornerstone of leadership was empathy, which meant looking at things from other perspectives. It was operating at three levels simultaneously – focusing on yourself, focusing on others and focusing on the wider world. Our meetings and interactions in our offices and with clients took on a different meaning. For me, it was to find out the true purpose of what we were doing. It was an incredible viewpoint, a feeling of liberation that swept over me.

From the myopic to the orbital

This dramatic shift of our point of view from local to global and myopic to orbital is the perspective we need today. Once again, I see the world in flux, the energy of motion, from my perch on the mountain top. But the patterns tell me of the coming of a great revolution. I saw the slim cellphone we hold in our hands transforming our civilization, from providing education to the remotest corners of our country to making the unbanked bankable in distant Africa. Connectivity is going to create a sustainable development model as we march ahead, and we are going to play a pivotal role in this.

Step back to take a panoramic view. You will see opportunities everywhere as we, as a country, and the world transform in the Fourth Industrial Revolution mentioned by Klaus Schwab. A revolution characterized by a host of new technologies to converge the physical, digital and biological worlds, impacting all disciplines, economies and industries. There will, of course, be pain in the process. Like the wildebeest that fall prey to the hungry crocodiles in the Mara River they had to cross with vultures swooping down on the carcasses of those who failed to make the crossing. Everyone was playing their own game of survival. Change is never an easy process and here we are talking about transformation – an upheaval on a scale the world hasn't witnessed before.

Our culture propagates the harmful myth that we should strive to be as comfortable as possible, to make life as pleasurable as possible and resist hardship as much as possible. No myth has made us unhappier as a people. Let's admit it: No one can be pleased or comfortable all the time. We can't control everything. Trying to achieve permanent comfort and control leads to a dull, meaningless existence that kills the soul.

As I watched the spectacular migration in Serengeti, what also struck me was that not everything was so peaceful as it appeared from my safe zone of observation. Some animals were too weak to make the journey and were falling behind; eventually, they would die. That was life – cruel and practical yet seeking a new start in a new land. The animals that were migrating were cutting their losses before it was too late to move on to better pastures. Of course, there was no guarantee that they would succeed but they had to take the risk.

Nature calls you back to reality. You can't stop it from raining. You can't delay the setting sun. You can't set the temperature to a comfortable 70 degrees Fahrenheit. If you've got a mountain to climb a mountain, your muscles are going to burn. There can be no motorable highway to the summit. But with this surrender comes such relief! It is like awakening from a dream to realize how little control we really have. You remember that hardship and lack of control are integral to life, and accepting this reality makes it not only bearable but allows us to sense the joy of being alive, realizing the larger purpose of what we do and feeling like a part of the Circle of Life.

Chapter 16

A Sudden Chance to Change the Status Quo

My life back home was going well. I was enjoying my work and felt like I was in full control of whatever I had been doing. My business calendar for the first half of 2020 was full of international travel and visits to several business schools as a keynote speaker. I was even trying to squeeze in an annual holiday to an exotic location with the family. All I needed to do was to shuffle a few dates to keep my commitments and fit in my agenda. Overall, a perfectly normal planner.

During a chilly late afternoon in February, I was in Barcelona and enjoying a hot coffee with a friend, sitting at a roadside café and gazing lazily at the passing crowd, when my cell phone rang. It was a person from the headquarters on the other end, suggesting that we start daily communication around the COVID-19 situation across all our locations in different countries. I sensed a tinge of anxiety in his voice as he talked about how we needed to ensure maintaining and delivering mission-critical activities of our customers should the virus spread beyond China.

COVID-19 wasn't news to me. Having an office in Wuhan along with several other places in China, I was actively involved in dealing with this crisis since January 2020. Our team there ensured that they would take all precautions, go under complete lockdown and work from home based on the government directives. Almost every other day, I was having Crisis Management meetings with our team in China to monitor the situation. Nevertheless, I still made a few calls from the café to our team and issued a few instructions.

I was about to return to India in two days. At that point in time, sitting in Barcelona, things didn't look alarming but certainly needed a close watch and a higher level of alertness on our part. Little did I think that Barcelona, Spain, the very place I was enjoying my coffee, would be one of the worst affected cities in the world in just a matter of weeks.

As I took the flight back to India, things looked normal. The airports, planes, passengers and the world around me moved at their usual pace. It was only a few weeks after my return to India that news started to trickle in dribs and drabs, and it didn't sound too good. The trickle soon turned into a torrent of ominous reports, and the world went topsy-turvy in a flash, blindsiding most of us. On March 11, 2020, the World Health Organization declared the rapidly spreading coronavirus outbreak as a pandemic, acknowledging what had seemed evident for some time – the virus would likely spread to all countries around the globe.

On March 24, within four hours' notice, the Indian prime minister announced that no one would be leaving home for 21 days – the most severe step taken anywhere in the war against the coronavirus till that point in time. All 1.3 billion people in the country were to stay indoors for three weeks – the biggest and most severe action undertaken to stop the spread of the coronavirus. Every state, district, lane and village would be under lockdown, the order proclaimed. The first phase of the lockdown, which was to be for 21 days, continued till June 1, 2020, spanning 68 days. Subsequent phases followed, although with fewer restrictions.

It may sound bizarre, but we were always wanting to change the world. Then suddenly, one fine morning, it happened. We pulled the handbrakes abruptly just when the pedal was about to hit the metal. Everything screeched to a grinding halt. The year 2020 had been a much-hyped milestone for the world; it symbolized perfect vision and somehow became futuristic in a phonetical way, pregnant with possibilities of hugely transformative technological advancements. In just a couple of weeks, the COVID-19 pandemic turned 2020 into *annus horribilis* (meaning 'Horrible Year' in Latin) from what was supposed to be *annus mirabilis*, which translated to the wonderful year. The world came to a standstill, life stopped and businesses switched off their lights and downed their shutters.

Uncertainty became the oft-repeated word by humanity, who were designed to be social animals. That very structure of our lives and business, which pivoted around working, living, meeting, traveling, dining, enjoying together in groups, just halted overnight. Physical distancing became the norm, masks covered our faces and we stopped shaking hands or hugging each other. Human touch itself became toxic. A few times during this period, when I had to go out for necessities, I could not recognize my city. Being in number 15 in the list of most populous cities in the world, Kolkata had turned into a ghost town. Nothing could have been more shocking.

Lives vs. Livelihoods

During the lockdown, economists were faced with the paradox of lives vs livelihoods. If we stayed home and quarantined ourselves, the virus stopped spreading but economic activities would collapse. If we went about our regular lives, we would become carriers of this deadly disease and people would die. At the time of writing this chapter, more than half-a-million people have died around the world.

Nearly six months into this crisis that has engulfed the entire world, we're now trying to tiptoe back to our normal lives. It is one step forward and two or even three steps backward. There were several false starts as the virus appeared to wane in its spread rate, only to resurge with even greater severity. Everyone now understood what flattening the curve meant. Epidemiologists, doctors and healthcare professionals were the heroes on the frontline, trying to save the world.

The amazing thing about humanity is its incredible resilience even when everything looks bleak and impossible. We pivoted around to turn the obstacles of uncertainty into opportunities. Organizations rapidly adapted to this uncertain world. Things that were supposed to have happened over a few years now took place within a couple of months or even weeks. We evolved to take these waves of uncertainties in our stride and made agility business as usual. Extreme flexibility became the standard feature of all our planning. Just when the world was grappling with the pandemic, the strongest cyclone in 100 years hit Kolkata. If nature was conspiring against humanity, then human nature could turn adversities into advantages.

A watershed moment when changes are permanent

Sometimes in life, we encounter watershed moments when things don't just change; they transform, mutate and metamorphose permanently. We are now passing through one such uncontrollable phase in our lives. The world is changing forever, and with it, our lives, livelihoods, the way we work and the skills we will need to endure the present without being overwhelmed. We must evolve with the transformations and redefine our skills and competencies to eventually emerge triumphant. It is an existential battle of our lifetimes and we don't have an option but to face it. At the same time, we have been also given the opportunity to change the status quo.

It is in this context that we need to analyze what these changes are, what it means to our lives and careers and how to equip ourselves to remain relevant in this new world order that is emerging. We must understand that what has worked before will not work now. COVID-19 demands physical distancing and operating remotely. When the telecom revolution started and India's outsourcing industry blossomed, we said, 'Geography is history'. By that, we meant distance had no significance now as work could be performed remotely from anywhere if one had connectivity.

Geography is History 2.0

This might be the second chapter of 'Geography is History' but in a more personalized way. In the late eighties and early nineties, we erased distances across continents. Now, we must create distances between ourselves to avoid physical proximity and stop the spread of this virus. This has created a new dimension in our economic activities – distance dynamics driven by remote everything in a contactless world.

So how do we carry out economic and social activities, like working together in offices, factories, meetings in cafes, watching movies, attending events or concerts, going to colleges and schools, visiting restaurants, shopping malls and markets, holidaying in exotic locations, flying in airplanes, traveling in trains and buses and living together in apartment blocks? Everything must be redesigned to create distances and be delivered remotely.

This has a cascading impact across industries ranging from retail, real estate, media and entertainment, event management, travel and tourism, education, manufacturing, hi-tech and telecommunication, banking and financial services, public sector, automobiles, shipping and transportation and pharma and healthcare. Some of these industries have been hit particularly hard while others relatively less so. The transformation would be painful and take time. However, no industry is insulated from this once-in-a-lifetime disruptive force, the effects of which will continue for at least the next five years. No one expected anything like this, with schools and colleges closed, global supply chains disrupted and millions of employees working from home. Even the Summer Olympics in Tokyo, which was scheduled for earlier this year, had to be postponed – an extremely rare decision.

Technologies like robotics, automation, remote surgery, telemedicine, telehealth, augmented and virtual reality, remote education, blockchain, internet of things, machine and deep learning, digital twins, 5G, edge computing and several others are now finding new use cases that were proving to be elusive before. Technologies that let us create economic value remotely or without the need for close physical contact will prosper and so would demand new skills associated with these. These are the technologies that will get a COVID-19 bump.

Some of these technologies were work-in-progress and were expected to mature and see adoption over the next three to four years, but distance dynamics have fast-forwarded the timeframe. It looks like the Fourth Industrial Revolution, which was to happen over the next few decades, has now telescoped into the next few years.

Opportunities in disruptions and creating demand for new skills

Large swathes of industries would be transformed and disrupted by some of these new technologies. It will also impact our professions in an inconceivable way. The need for physical distancing will drive automation in industries. There will be new opportunities that will explode in the COVID-19 world. While a lot of careers and jobs are getting destroyed, new ones are being generated. Every economic downturn, war or other similar crisis has seen the 'bunching' of innovations and then a sudden unleashing of new technologies once the challenging times are over.

As most companies were scrambling to get Work From Home (WFH) systems in place, a few global technology organizations had already been preparing to implement this as a business as usual practice to optimize costs, cut down on carbon footprint and adapting themselves to allow employees to create economic value from anywhere. These organizations rapidly pivoted around to meet the exigencies of COVID-19. In a way, they transformed to become location agnostic. Employees could be anywhere and still tethered to the virtual hubs nearby, having full access to enterprise resources in a highly secure environment and collaborating with teammates through sophisticated platforms using mixed reality, which gave a feeling of almost being there. It will allow companies a fantastic opportunity to expand their pool from which to recruit the best talent as locations would no longer be a constraint.

The technology companies had been preparing to adopt automation, seamless collaboration platforms and implement new technologies. They were already investing in increasing the security of their digital assets and intellectual property in this new environment. So when the pandemic hit hard, they did not find themselves as completely blindsided as some others. In my own organization, it was amazing to see how HR functions could quickly move into a virtual onboarding of new employees. From interviewing to onboarding to training to deployment on projects, everything is now seamlessly happening without going to the office. I could not have visualized this some 12 months back. Video collaboration is at its best.

The other day, a friend of mine was arguing about the relevance of advanced technologies during such a crisis period. A couple of reports had caught his attention over the last few months. They described how AI was failing to forecast things during the pandemic. We talked in length and it became clear the reason was that AI needed lots of past data to run its predictive engines. COVID-19, being a once-in-a-century event, didn't have past data. It was a key reason why AI programs were not working as expected. With large swathes of the world population staying at home, normal life has hit the pause button. People's routines, needs and priorities are changing every day. And marketers are feeling the effects as their plans are being thrown out of the window. Switching to an unscripted marketing model calls for more insight into the shifting consumer mindset and that's a moving target now.

Retailers faced a major information deficit when the global lockdown happened as customer interactions over the counter dried up. That's a big problem because a robust flow of that information is the lifeblood of customer loyalty programs, AI-driven product recommendations and a range of mission-critical business decisions. The data-to-decision process has been severely disrupted across industries – from hotels and tourism to automobiles, retail, education and other sectors that also depend on person-to-person contact and generating information.

This would mean that what worked BC (Before Coronavirus) won't work PC (Post-COVID) future. We, therefore, need to question our basic assumptions about everything and figure out opportunities that no one has yet seen. The basic architectures of our businesses, e.g., supply chain, must be created afresh on a clean slate. What has worked before is now creating barriers like our workspace infrastructures. With almost 100% of employees working from home, organizations are bearing the burden of idle real estate.

So it's not going to be a question of restarting things from where we paused but rather starting anew on a fresh slate. It's a huge opportunity and a challenge at the same time. The best part is that no one can tell us that this was how it has always been done. What has worked before won't work now or tomorrow.

If one analyses the first three industrial revolutions, one would notice that technology was mostly replacing or augmenting human physical or mental efforts. By sharp contrast, the Fourth Industrial Revolution was ushering in a cyber-physical era in which physical objects were being embedded with cyber properties. If physical things were atoms and bits defined the cyber world, then bits and atoms were coming together for the first time, getting connected and creating new value. Technology was being used to mimic human intellectual capability of thinking, laying the foundation of artificial reasoning in the not-too-distant future.

This would transform the future of work and even leadership will be disrupted in Industry 4.0, which will witness highly advanced human-machine interfaces, enabling faster, better automation paired with the power of the human brain. Elon Musk's Neuralink is already working on advanced brain-computer links.

If individuals must keep pace with these shifts to avoid redundancy, business leaders are faced with the daunting task of the overabundance of emerging technologies in the market, all with promises to revolutionize the way businesses operate. From AI and machine learning to IoT, 5G, 3D manufacturing and blockchain, the list is endless.

This is also transforming the nature of work itself. Skills are becoming redundant at the speed of thought. Customer preferences are changing at the tap of an icon in their smartphones and the shelf life of ideas is as perishable as a carton of milk. Established companies are being challenged by nimble start-ups. Technological innovations are disrupting the market dominance of powerful enterprises. While these changes require new thoughts and ideas to move ahead, at the same time, they also need us to revisit the basics lessons of life.

Things that our schools should teach

Trust, Transparency, Empathy are timeless qualities. As I have repeatedly said in the previous chapters, to me, compassion is perhaps the single more important quality in a human being. Not only in our personal relationships, but empathy will also always help us better understand other points of view. In an increasingly connected world, collaboration will be the key to success. It will require us to understand our colleagues, customers and partners from across the world.

We will have to overcome cultural barriers, prejudices and respect diversity in all its forms. Empathy will be the cornerstone of everything we will do. It is the most essential thing to consider while designing products and services for our customers. Conflict resolution is another important trait that is required in our professional lives as much as in our personal lives. I wish there was a lesson on conflict resolution at school. Here, I have tried to list six things that, in my opinion, every school should teach:

- Public speaking
- Customer service
- Critical thinking
- People management
- Conflict resolution
- How to handle failure

These are skills that can never be automated. As skills shift continuously in the ever-changing landscape of technology, we need to focus on getting the basics right, which would see us through any disruption or transformation. Critical thinking is about asking the right questions and spending time analyzing problems before leaping into solutions.

Critical thinking, people management and empathy put together is the ideal combination for conflict resolution. Empathy helps one to understand the other points of view and figure out the trigger points behind it. Proper people management skills allow people the freedom to express their views candidly without being judgmental. In self-managing teams, conflicts are resolved within the teams itself and rarely need to be escalated upwards. A culture of open communication can turn conflict resolution into a group activity that can unleash the creativity of its members.

Perhaps the most important lesson our schools and other academic institutions need to teach is how to handle failure. Do I remember the day I came back from school, taking a long, long time to trudge back the same path, head hung in shame, with a poor report card in the satchel? Do we remember the rejection letter from a prestigious university we threw away so that others wouldn't see it? Do we recall the day when we came back from the office, having missed a promotion? We put up a brave front and never talked about it.

During the 2008 Financial Meltdown, people who lost their jobs never shared their stories with their families. Some of them dressed up every morning and left home, pretending to go to work as usual. Instead, they went to coffee shops or parks, logged on and sent out their CVs, looking for another job. We are all afraid of failure. It's a social dishonor, a humiliation, a shame.

I looked back at the years of my life that I have lived. It struck me that most of it wasn't about being successful. A lot of it was about rejections, disappointments, dejections and failures. Like the tip of an iceberg, the world looks at the measures of external success in our corporate titles, the businesses, the cars we drive, the houses we live in and, nowadays, the mirroring of our lives on social media. If there were any means of dissecting our lives by success and failure, I am sure that a larger slice of our lives would be about not achieving what we set out to rather than achieving it. It can be as heartbreaking as your parents not buying you a bicycle in your teens or missing out on a raise that you felt you deserved after all that hard work.

Let's look at some shocking data. The annual figure of suicide rates by students in India turned out to be the highest in a decade – over 10,000 in 2018. Twenty-eight students on average committed suicide every 24 hours in the same year, according to National Crime Records Bureau data. They were the victims of a system that has not trained us to handle setbacks. As a nation and a society, we are unforgiving about failures.

This is perhaps one of the reasons why we have performed so miserably when it comes to innovation. Once again, let's examine crucial data – the number of patents. India has an old reputation: It remains a minnow when it comes to patents. If over 600,000 applications were filed in the US and more than twice that number in China in 2017, in India, there were only 46,600. Patent grants came to just over 12,000 in a country of 1.37 billion people, according to a report in The Economic Times, published last year.

Shikhar Ghosh, a senior lecturer at Harvard Business School sums up the situation perfectly. "In any natural system, failure is the engine that causes growth, that causes new birth, that causes anything to happen," he says. "One of the truly big differences between growing economies and economies that stagnate is the acceptance of failure."

We all like to glamorize failure stories of Steve Jobs or Bill Gates getting turned down by IBM and even Amitabh Bachchan having 12 consecutive flops before his first super hit, *Zanjeer*, his business getting wiped off and his subsequent triumph with KBC. We all applaud such turnaround stories yet the stigma of failure carries on. It is an albatross that hangs around our necks.

My lesson from life is that failure happens when we chase success. This is what raises expectations and when most of those aren't fulfilled, we term it as a failure. If for a moment we stepped back and said that the outcome of our efforts should be creating value, then success would be a default outcome. Value creation is a continuous process. There are no failures in this progression. Each step is an incremental success.

Throughout our lives, we are trying to avoid failure like a plague and every single person on the planet has failed. Every single successful person on the planet has failed and made something of it. Sadly, however, we aren't trained to appreciate this process. Let's put failure in the syllabus. It will be even more relevant today, as we adjust to this volatile, ambiguous and complex world. Life looks so different in just a few months.

How life looks from here

All of us are now in our own corners of home offices, connected to each other through a network that includes even the CXOs. It is a fact that we won't get back to the past normal even when the threat of COVID-19 retreats. This will of course lead to a reassessment of roles and responsibilities. Team sizes will become much smaller as, otherwise, remote management will not be possible. Outcome-based management will replace the current industrial age managerial practices that depend on the physical supervision of the employees to ensure completion of tasks. This model will need highly empowered employees to deliver. Supervision will automatically become less important in this scenario.

In this outcome-based model, teams will become flexible and so will leadership roles be within teams. Teams with the right skills to execute a project will be quickly assembled and a leader assigned to manage the project. Once this delivery is completed, the teams will be disbanded and skills redistributed within the organization. A leader in one team can become a member of another team, depending on the skills required for that project. Skills will no longer belong to a single business unit but will be available for deployment to the entire organization.

Enterprises will focus on putting employees on a continuous learning mode to stay abreast of the latest technological developments. Large parts of our work will be digitized as we discover new ways of connecting through collaborative platforms while working remotely. Automation will take center stage. This will also enhance the pace of Robotic Process Automation with minimal human intervention. We will also see more human-machine collaboration as humans become even more skilled to operate systems remotely and gain a higher comfort level with far more sophisticated human-machine interfaces. This will speed up Augmented Intelligence where human skills will be augmented by machine capabilities.

Remote everything would be the new mantra. Skills like remote surgery, remote teaching, learning how to learn remotely and autonomous operations will be in higher demand, essentially spurred by our experience of functioning in a contactless environment. The cybersecurity challenges of working from home or remotely will throw up new challenges that will need to enhance the security of the devices we use, known as end-point security, which protects the final gadget we use to access our office IT systems and organizational networks.

We will figure out that having a lot of meetings is not a sign of being productive. There are so many such meetings that can now be avoided. This will increase our productivity. Data from the past few months are proving it to be so. We are already seeing the rise of the 30-minute meeting.

Last but not the least, we will learn to travel less. Existing client relationships will need to be strengthened over the digital space, using highly enhanced AR and VR collaborative tools. This will also save one of the biggest expense line items in the corporate budgets.

The future of work has arrived – together apart

A caged box contraption costing $300 and moving at about 20 cm per second was a technological innovation that transformed cityscapes and gave us our offices of today. The world's first successful safe passenger elevator was designed by Elisha Otis and installed in March 1857 at the five-story, 24-meter tall, Haughwout Building on Broadway, New York City. It transformed cities, workspaces and our lives.

Cityscapes of metropolises from Mumbai to New York, Dubai or Shanghai have always been defined by silhouettes of their glass and aluminum skyscrapers, symbolizing the power of their global enterprises. The offices in those tall structures radiated the energy and influence of the organizations, which spread across the world. People who inhabited the cubicles and the rows of neat desks inside bathed themselves in that same energy and authority. They were the ones who shaped the ebb and tide of economic currents around the planet.

The COVID-19 pandemic has struck a sledgehammer blow to these very edifices, rocking their foundations. The offices that we know today have been de-populated as over 90% of employees are now working from home. The hub of power and glory that was so central to our professional existence, satisfying our sense of belonging to a club, meeting our physiological needs of stable employment, connectivity, shelter and giving us the warm and fuzzy feeling of esteem and prestige of working in urbane workspaces no longer exists in the shape and form we knew it for so long.

The pandemic is having a similar and as powerful an impact as that generated by the Otis elevator. It has had three significant effects – it is questioning the need for a physical office, at least the kind we have now; it is redefining work; it has opened a torrent of technological transformations. We have been talking about the future of work for quite some time, and suddenly, the Future Is Now, all-pervasive and encompassing everything around us. Technological transformations that should have happened over the next five years have been compacted into the last four months.

Chapter 17

Building India Next

"Things change every day. With each new dawn, it is not the same world as before. And you're not the same person you were either." – Haruki Murakami, *Kafka on the Shore*

***

Murakami's simplicity makes him one of my favorite authors. The above quote is perhaps strikingly germane today than ever before. The world has been made unrecognizable as the pandemic hit us from early 2020. It will never be the same again, but I also have my own version of life. The more things change, the more they remain the same.

During a storm, ships drop anchors and boats look for a buoy to tie itself to. I am a boy from the banks of the river Ganga, the prime distributary of which is christened Hooghly as it flows past Kolkata, touching the banks of Barrackpore on the way. When I was a kid, growing up in Barrackpore in the northern suburbs of the metropolis, the river ran deep. Large vessels plied along with smaller fishing boats; they still do. I remember the shining catch of silvery Hilsa, the ultimate local delicacy, unloaded on the banks of the river. I still make time to visit my childhood friends who live there. Every morning, the boats and vessels bring in their catch of the day even now. The anchors and buoys continue to keep the vessels from drifting away.

Our values, visions and principles are like these anchors that become even more relevant as the hurricane of an uncertain future rages around us. These are what keeps us moored to the basic lessons of life that will continue to support us in these turbulent times. Things have changed beyond recognition since my childhood days. Our lives have been transformed over the last four decades and will continue to change, but the values we lived our lives by will never change. We will be different persons in many ways, but deep within us, these will remain untouched. We are never the same, but life has shaped us to become better versions of ourselves. In that sense, Murakami is correct.

My anchors in life

Whatever little I have achieved, I owe to some amazing people in my life who have held my hand, coached, guided and mentored me. Had it not been for Prof. Samir Sadhukhan's candid and sincere advice that I should give up trying to get into an engineering college and instead learn coding to solve problems, I wouldn't have even started this journey. He taught me something more important – the value of selflessness. He showed me the importance of helping others to succeed. I can't still forget how he traveled all the way from Kolkata in an unreserved compartment of the Indian Railways to Ganjam in Odisha to help me with a project I was stuck with. This is the only leadership mantra one needs to learn – make others successful.

Even my manager in St Louis, Mississippi, US, showed me with his unreasonableness that it was important to look at things from the other person's perspective. It became the cornerstone of my approach to life and work. I never hated him but tried to fathom why he disliked me and how I could set things right. I learned that one should never quit when the chips are down but decide what you have to do when you're on a high. The resignation letter I wrote when life was looking impossible stayed in my pocket. It was a sort of a reminder for me to keep at it till such time they realized that my work was indispensable.

Rejections are part of life

It was in St Louis that I realized that life would be unfair. Disappointments and rejections are all part of life. Unfairness is built into society but that didn't mean I would be unfair to others. I couldn't because I understood how hurtful it could be to a person. Later in life, when times were tough and difficult decisions needed to be taken that would affect the life and livelihoods of others, I looked back at St Louis and decided that I had to be fair. I didn't need to change but became aware of the realities of life and navigated accordingly.

When my first IT outsourcing project in Nepal looked as if I had been given something that was destined for failure and I was to perform the last rites, I realized how to focus on small achievements. I didn't have experience in project management; this was baptism by fire. Even the most daunting pieces of work appear less if one takes time to analyze the problems, break it up into smaller components and solve each at a time. The only thing one can do in a crisis is to take one day at a time, each piece at a time, bit by bit until the picture is completed.

My middle-class upbringing, humble academic background and lessons of selflessness all taught me that life was about making the right choices – choices that were humane and good for people. They weren't perfect choices but doing the right things is better than doing things right. Doing things right meant following every punctuation of well-laid-out processes even if it meant being dispassionate toward people. I have been in situations when following processes and doing things right could have been the safest course of action for my career. However, it was always the tougher choice of doing the right things that made sense to me, and eventually, it proved to be good for the organization because it was good for people. You can't go wrong with choosing the right thing to do instead of doing things right.

An opportunity for India next

Today, I am as excited as I was on the flight back from San Francisco. Then, it was because of the opportunities I could see in front of us – driving the frugal innovation and making India a strong force in information technology on the world map.

Today, the health crisis has created an economic emergency and that, in turn, is producing geopolitical tensions. This is an opportunity for India to position itself as a key player in the new supply chains that will emerge. To ride this opportunity, we must first focus on building talent, equipping them with the skills that are required for today. Our education curriculum needs to be oriented toward creating talent that is focused on creativity, ingenuity and innovation. It cannot be the old system of cramming in at coaching centers and pouring it out in exam halls. An overhaul of the education system is a must first step.

Our education system must teach students about the Fourth Industrial Revolution and how it is changing the world. The skills that will be required to survive and thrive in this revolution is different from the old. Digital dexterity will be a must for everyone. It must begin from our primary school levels. Today's digital native generation has the brains to learn these skills as they intuitively operate a smartphone or remote controller without being trained. Unless the workforce is transformed with digital skills, there will be large scale unemployment resulting from technological redundancy.

If India is to offer itself as a vital node in the architecture of the new supply chains, then it cannot waste time in building afresh. Rather, it has to use its existing strengths. We have Indian companies like Bajaj, IFB, TVS, ISRO, Amul and their likes who make globally competitive products. Let's look for such companies and create an environment for them to become international players. Some of them are already global, but with government help, they can become an even more powerful force in the international arena. MNCs and Indian IT companies have also built a huge reservoir of experience in operating within a global supply chain.

The government must foster an environment where they will provide the impetus to make this transformation and act as shock absorbers to help these enterprises make this change. You must understand that one cannot become a global player in the new supply chain without being technologically advanced. We cannot any longer compete on price, but we must work on quality, delivery timelines and also have a competitive pricing strategy. The big shift from low-priced to competitive pricing based on superior quality is a must. To do this, investment in R&D, technology and training are essential.

I can visualize a troika ecosystem of 'small firms big players research institutes' creating India Next. We have proven to the world with our IT prowess, and now, it is time again to use this crisis to reboot India into a global supply chain node. When I returned to India over two decades ago, I did so out of a conviction that it was the place to be in. It was poised for greatness. Today, it is time to recreate our magic once again. We can do it if we learn to accept failure, take each day at a time, focus on delivering excellence and not chase winning all the time, use empathy to understand what the global consumer needs, play fairly with integrity, ensure the success of our customers-partners-employees and invest in the technologies of tomorrow. It is not difficult; let's break up the challenges into smaller pieces and encourage merit, and we will be respected worldwide as we have always been. Ours is a beautiful, peace-loving country that welcomes everyone. Let's use this to rediscover our mojo. Now is the time to do it.

Chapter 18

The Story of the Second Arrow

Buddha once asked a student, "If a person is struck by an arrow, is it painful? If the person is struck by a second arrow, is it even more painful?" He then went on to explain, "In life, we cannot always control the first arrow. However, the second arrow is our reaction to the first. There will always be a second arrow coming after the first one, and with this second arrow comes the possibility of choice."

While the Coronavirus hitting us is the first arrow, the second arrow is the anxiety and worry over our near and dear ones as well as the financial crisis that will happen. These are the thoughts that cloud our minds and create confusion in our actions. The only way to blunt the impact of the second arrow is to train our minds to think of positive things that are in our control. It is useless to worry about what we cannot control; let's focus on what we can. That is resilience!

If today, it is the virus that is creating uncertainties, five years ago, it was technology that was triggering the volatility around us. COVID-19 is just another uncertain event that happened. The mind becomes resilient when we accept uncertainty as a part of our lives. The thought that things are functioning normally and with dead certainty is quite strange. Just ponder for once that the Earth under our feet is only a boiling mass of rocks and lava deep within. The oceans around us are violent. The Earth itself is a tiny blue dot that barely escapes getting hit by thousands of asteroids every second.

Uncertainty is more a part of life than certainty. Be it one of the managers we could not make happy, be it not getting that promotion or losing that most important project or yet another unpredictable event causing severe disruption to our lives and livelihoods – events like 9/11, the 2008 Financial Meltdown and so on. Our preparedness in accepting such unexpected to happen is what it means to be resilient. It is the capacity of an individual or a company to absorb stress, recover critical functionality and thrive in altered circumstances.

We must refuse to be beaten down by adversities. We must keep coming back stronger, redefine our strengths to meet new challenges and have the grit of repeating them again and again. We cannot avoid the first arrow but the second one is in our control.

Epilogue: Mississippi Morphs into Ganga

I had trouble managing the S's and p's while spelling Mississippi in my early days at St Louis, Missouri. It took me a bit of practice to get it right. The river was just five miles from where I lived. It attracted me like a magnet. I missed the river of my childhood, and the shores of the Mississippi was where I wanted to be. It was as if to seek solace from someone familiar. I could sense a connection with the mighty Ganga and this massive body of water that flowed 3700 kilometers, draining all or parts of 31 US states and nearly 40% of the landmass of the United States.

The Ganga flowed through Barrackpore, a sleepy satellite town in the northern outskirts of the great metropolis of Kolkata, where my childhood and significant parts of my youth were spent. The river was entwined in our lives. It was our playground as we frolicked in its muddy waters. This was where we got our first lessons in swimming and sinking from disciplinarian elders in the family. The process was simple yet highly effective – literally being thrown into the river! Boy, how quickly we learned to keep our heads above water.

EPILOGUE

The cool breeze that blew over the Ganga soothed our sweat-drenched bodies after a boisterous, muddy game of football. Its shores were the solace of our youth, where we gathered around in the evenings for a cigarette with our buddies, to share our tales of loves, heartbreaks and dreams. There were no nightmares then. Everything seemed doable with the abundance of energy and the incurable innocence of adolescence. If we could learn to swim in this mighty river, we could do anything. The river flowed through our arteries.

With the first harsh taste of realism in St Louis, I longed for the river of my youth. I longed for its comforting breeze and the cool lap of its waters on my body. For me, the Mississippi and the Ganga merged into one during the lonely, desperate days at St Louis, where I was learning my new lessons in life. Once again, it felt like being tutored to swim the hard way – by being dumped into the river of reality. However, it took my wife and me almost a year to save enough to take a riverboat cruise down the Mississippi. As we sailed along the river in the paddle boat, along the famous Gateway Arch, the immense power of the Mississippi struck me.

At the same time, I felt that if I could learn to swim in the Ganga in Barrackpore, I could do it here in the US of America as well. The cloudy waters looked just the same. Much like the river back home, which created the massive Gangetic plains as it coursed its way from the mighty Himalayas to the murky forests of Sundarbans in the eastern coast of India where it merged into the Bay of Bengal. The Mississippi, too, was the lifeline of the American states. The resemblances were striking. The energy of the Mississippi seeped into me; everything seemed possible. The nightmares started to fade. My fears appeared inconsequential.

I looked at the waters churned by the paddles of the steamboat, and in a moment of realization, I understood how the river stayed calm and serene despite all our efforts to agitate it. The energy generated by the paddles whipping the waters was as much necessary as the placidity of massive waterbody that flowed at its own pace amidst the chaos. That was life – staying calm when things around us turned topsy-turvy.

I gazed at the horizon as evening tiptoed over the river. Beginning as a trickle out of Lake Itasca in northern Minnesota, this river flows a full 3700 kilometers until it pours into the Gulf of Mexico below New Orleans, like the Ganga, which cheerfully tumbles down from the steep Himalayas to morph into a deep tranquil flow as it reaches the plains. Life, too, followed the same contours, gathering experiences along the way only to mellow down as maturity dawns.

Just like a river, life meets obstacles on its way and learns how to skirt around and continue with its journey. It is for the river to nourish the terrain through which it flows. Such was the purpose of our lives too – to sustain and enrich the lives of those around us. When the river floods, it deposits rich soils and creates a diverse ecology. Similarly, our lives would be meaningless unless we create an ecosystem of empathy and relationships where everyone contributes toward a common goal. A river doesn't try to win or lose; it simply flows. Life isn't about winning or being successful; it is about enjoying the flow, enriching everyone encountered on the way and staying on course till the end.

Talking about the Mississippi River and not mentioning Samuel Langhorne Clemens, more famous by his pen name, Mark Twain, who started life as a riverboat pilot in this river, is like trying to describe the Ganga without the spirit of India. In his famous book *Life on the Mississippi*, Twain describes his lessons in navigating the unpredictable and ever-changing shape of the river. At times, it differed between morning and night. His boss, the captain of the steamboat, Mr. Bixby, had a warm core with a tough exterior.

Every time apprentice Twain felt that he had managed to pack his head full of islands, towns, bars, 'points' and bends and was confident enough to sail to New Orleans on his own, a torrent of expletives from the captain would rudely ground the young apprentice to reality. After one such stormy outburst, Captain Bixby explained calmly, "My boy, you've got to know the shape of the river perfectly. It is all there is left to steer by on a very dark night. Everything else is blotted out and gone. But mind you, it hasn't the same shape in the night that it has in the day-time."

As I look at the mayhem around us today, I notice that everything is changing around with unprecedented velocity. The Next has suddenly become the Now. We are all riverboat pilots today, taking each day at a time, learning, unlearning and relearning how to navigate the rapidly ever-changing landscape. I have seen how the Ganga by my small hometown changes course, creates new islands, breaks shores and defines a new route for itself. That is how we need to follow the river of our times – unhurried yet keeping pace with things. Understanding the transformative forces at play that disrupt our present will define our future. All the while, the core values of our principles will keep flowing – unchanged and forever.

www.ingramcontent.com/pod-product-compliance
Lightning Source LLC
Chambersburg PA
CBHW030938180526
45163CB00002B/614